Love Is the Measure

Love Is the Measure

A Biography of Dorothy Day

Revised Edition

JIM FOREST

ORBIS BOOKS

Maryknoll, New York 10545

The Catholic Foreign Mission Society of America (Maryknoll) recruits and trains people for overseas missionary service. Through Orbis Books, Maryknoll aims to foster the international dialogue that is essential to mission. The books published, however, reflect the opinions of their authors and are not meant to represent the official position of the society.

Copyright © 1986, 1994 by James H. Forest
Originally published by Paulist Press, 997 Macarthur Blvd., Mahwah, N.J. 07430

This revised edition published by Orbis Books, Maryknoll, NY 10545

Manufactured in the United States of America

Library of Congress Cataloging-in-Publication

Forest, James H.
    Love is the measure : a biography of Dorothy Day / Jim Forest.
        p.   cm.
    Originally published: New York, N.Y. : Paulist Press, © 1986.
    Includes bibliographical references and index.
    ISBN 0-88344-942-0 (pbk.)
    1. Day, Dorothy, 1897-1980.   2. Catholics—United States—
Biography.   3. Social reformers—United States—Biography.
4. Catholic Worker Movement.   I. Title.
BX4705.D283F67   1994
267'.182'09—dc20
    [B]   93-41162
                                                                   CIP

To my father,
who was among those to receive
the first issue of *The Catholic Worker*
on Union Square, May Day, 1933

Contents

Acknowledgments

I am indebted to a number of people active in the Catholic Worker movement who read all or part of this book while it was in manuscript and gave timely advice about ways to correct or improve the text, and to others who found errors following the book's first publication in 1986.

Most especially, my thanks go to Tom and Monica Cornell. Monica was born into a Catholic Worker family, while Tom was drawn to the Catholic Worker while a college student, after reading Dorothy Day's autobiography, *The Long Loneliness*. Many of my favorite stories about Dorothy come from Tom and Monica. Their Catholic Worker vocations continue; after founding Guadalupe House in Waterbury, Connecticut, and remaining with it for many years, they have "retired" to the Catholic Worker farm community in Marlborough, New York. (Now Tom and I are re-editing our *Catholic Worker* anthology, *A Penny a Copy*, first published in 1968, which Orbis Books will shortly publish.)

Robert Ellsberg has been another major help. He and I were the two youngest managing editors *The Catholic Worker* ever had, though Robert was longer at the job than I. While writing this book, it was an immense help having at my disposal the manuscript of Robert's anthology, *Dorothy Day: Selected Writings*. His introduction provides one of the best essays on Dorothy. Through Robert, I was able to see Dorothy in her last years, when I was living on the other side of the Atlantic Ocean.

Pat Jordan and Peggy Scherer, former editors of *The Catholic Worker*, also read the manuscript and gave valuable advice.

Phillip Runkel, responsible for the Catholic Worker archives at the Marquette University Memorial Library, again and again found papers I needed, and has since spotted several errors in the first edition which are, thanks to him, not to be found in the second edition. Never has an archivist been more committed not only to the papers in his care but to the spiritual values they represent.

The late Fritz Eichenberg, whose wood engravings and drawings are well known to every reader of *The Catholic Worker*, shared with me his extensive correspondence with Dorothy. His Catholic Worker art has recently been published by Orbis Books in an exceptionally handsome book: *Fritz Eichenberg Works of Mercy*. Not every *Catholic Worker* reader could read the articles, but even the most unlettered person could understand what the paper stood for thanks to Fritz Eichenberg's art.

Bill Barrett, on the staff of the New York Catholic Worker house late in Dorothy's life, was a helpful correspondent and also the source of some wonderful photos of Dorothy. He was one of the few photographers who didn't make her nervous.

Peter Hebblethwaite, biographer of Popes John XXIII and Paul VI, was helpful in the section of this book that involves John XXIII.

That this book appeared in the first place is thanks to Don Brophy, managing editor at Paulist Press, and that it appears in a new, revised edition is thanks to Robert Ellsberg, editor-in-chief at Orbis.

Finally, I must thank this book's widwife, my wife Nancy. Worse things could happen to a writer than to be married to an editor.

JIM FOREST
Alkmaar, Holland
October 10, 1993

May Day

A clear contralto voice filled Union Square in New York with the words, *"Arise, ye workers of the world."* In moments 50,000 were singing together the Communist hymn. *"Arise, ye wretched of the earth."* Tears sparkled in the eyes of those whom editorial writers sometimes described as godless, heartless and witless radicals. *"For Justice thunders condemnation."* Large numbers of police, some on horseback, watched from the sidelines of the huge crowd. *"A better world's in birth."*

It was May Day, 1933. Franklin Delano Roosevelt had been in the White House only a hundred days. The Great Depression was in its fourth year. Industrial production was barely half what it had been in 1929. More than 13,000,000 workers were unemployed. The majority of America's banks had collapsed, while those which survived were busily repossessing houses, shops and farms whose owners couldn't make mortgage payments. Hoovervilles—shantytowns for the homeless made of tin, cardboard and scrapwood—had sprung up in vacant lots all over the country. There was no Social Security program. Mickey Mouse was five years old. Hitler was the new chancellor of Germany.

The speakers at Union Square denounced Hitler and the Depression and called for worker ownership and control of industry. Despite hard times, their audience was in a festive mood. There were brass bands, red flags, and faces that were hopeful about the future, as if to say, "Perhaps in my lifetime the revolution will happen. Perhaps America's economic structures will be as democratic as its political philosophy."

One of those present, Dorothy Day, remembered that the square was filled with "a hot undulant sea of hats and sun-baked heads, over which floated a disordered array of banners, placards and pennants." But Dorothy Day wasn't carrying a placard or paying attention to the speeches. She was one of four people handing out the first issue of an eight-page tabloid newspaper, *The Catholic Worker*, and wasn't even asking for its cover price, a penny a copy. (An Irishman objected that a "penny" was an English coin, and therefore was far too much to ask.)

She found more bewilderment than enthusiasm from those who had the paper thrust into their hands. They knew *The Daily Worker*, a Communist paper, a militant supporter of unions and strikes. But a radical paper put

1

out by *Catholics*? Everyone knew that the Catholic Church was far more anti-Communist than pro-worker.

Many copies of the first *Catholic Worker* found their way onto the ground or into the nearest trash barrel. But some were read and seen as a welcome sign that a fresh wind was blowing in the Catholic Church.

A page-one editorial written by Dorothy Day, but unsigned, declared this new paper was published "for those who are huddling in shelters trying to escape the rain, for those who are walking the streets in the all but futile search for work, for those who think that there is no hope for the future, no recognition of their plight."

The Catholic Worker would let its readers know "that the Catholic Church has a social program" and that there are people of God "who are working not only for their spiritual, but for their material welfare."

"The fundamental aim of most radical sheets is the conversion of their readers to radicalism and atheism.

"Is it not possible to be radical and not an atheist? Is it not possible to protest, to expose, to complain, to point out abuses and demand reforms without desiring the overthrow of religion?"

The editorial boasted of the paper's fragile economic foundations: "The first number of *The Catholic Worker* was planned, written and edited in the kitchen of a tenement on 15th Street, on subway platforms, on the 'El' [elevated train], on the ferry. There is no editorial office, no overhead in the way of telephone or electricity, no salaries paid." The $57 cost of printing 2,500 copies of the first issue was paid by a few small contributions, plus the editors' savings, and what could be spared by not paying gas and electric bills. "By accepting delay, the utilities did not know that they were furthering the cause of social justice. . . .

"It is cheering to remember that Jesus Christ wandered this earth with no place to lay his head. '*The foxes have holes and the birds of the air their nests, but the Son of Man has no place to lay his head.*' And when we consider our fly-by-night existence, our uncertainty, we remember (with pride in sharing the honor) that the disciples supped by the seashore and wandered through cornfields picking the ears from the stalks wherewith to make their frugal meals."

Who were "the editors" who had delayed paying their bills? At the time, it was really just one person, Dorothy Day, thirty-five years old.

From Brooklyn to California

Dorothy Day was born November 8, 1897, at a house on Pineapple Street in Brooklyn Heights, not far from the Brooklyn Bridge. The third of the Day children, she had been preceded by Donald in 1895 and Sam Houston in 1896. Two others followed Dorothy: Della in 1899 and John in 1912. All but Della grew up to become journalists, with Sam Houston Day ending his career as managing editor of *The New York Journal American*, a right-wing paper that featured crime news.

Their father, John Day, was a newspaperman as well, whose specialty was the race track. He was born in Tennessee in 1870, was of Scotch-Irish descent, liked whiskey, and disliked foreigners, blacks and radicals. He was a religious skeptic, although he often quoted the Bible and, Dorothy remembered, "carried one with him always." Later in his life, he wrote a racing column, "On and Off the Turf," for *The New York Morning Telegraph*. For a time he was an inspector for the New York State Racing Commission, and later a steward and partner of the Hialeah race track in Florida. It may be that he found it easier to be with horses than with his children, at least with Dorothy. In her autobiographical writings, he emerges as a shadowy, unsympathetic figure, irritated with the intrusion of children into his marriage. He was deeply disapproving of the direction Dorothy took in life in both faith and politics. When the children ate Sunday dinner in the company of their parents, Dorothy found it a grim event. "None spoke; all ate in gloomy silence. . . . We could hear each other swallow." Because of him, it was a family in which "there was never any kissing, and never a close embrace."

His wife, Grace Satterlee, is remembered by Dorothy with grateful affection. She had been born in Marlboro, New York, in the Hudson Valley, in 1870. One wing of the family had gone to sea, and in a particular generation nine brothers had been captains of whalers and all but one been lost. The one survivor was Christian Satterlee, who married Charity Hummel-Washburn, Dorothy Day's great-grandmother. Christian had nearly died under sail. "He fell from a mast," Dorothy wrote, "and cracked his head and was never quite right after that, running down Delafield Street in his night shirt and finally drowning in a brook." He lasted long enough to father Napoleon Bonaparte Satterlee, who went off to fight in the Civil War, returning home from a prison camp with a damaged larynx. For the rest of his life he only spoke in a hoarse whisper which he treated with eggnog brought to him by his daughter Grace, or Graceful, as he preferred to call her.

Grace delighted in telling her children stories of what it was like when she was a little girl and who was in the family before she was born. "How we loved these stories," Dorothy wrote, "and how welcome our warm house was as we heard of terrible winters with the Hudson freezing over so that skating and ice-boating was commonplace." Such stories gave her "a sense of continuity."

While a student at Eastman's Business School in New York City, Grace Satterlee met John Day and soon after they were married at the Perry Street Episcopal Church in Greenwich Village. Within a year, Donald was born, and Dorothy two years later.

Dorothy's first six years were lived in Brooklyn. "I can remember well the happy hours on the beach with my brothers, and fishing in the creeks for eel, and running away with a younger cousin to an abandoned shack in a waste of swamp around Fort Hamilton, and pretending we were going to live there all by ourselves."

"On one occasion I went away all alone," Dorothy recalled of an early experiment with solitude, "spending what I felt to be long hours one sunny afternoon, blissful enchanted hours until the sudden realization came over me that I was alone, and the world was vast and that there were evil forces therein . . . then suddenly the black fear overwhelmed me at being alone, so that I ran all the way home."

Her last year in Brooklyn was her first year in school. "We prayed . . . every morning, bowing our heads on our desks and saying the Our Father, and I can still smell the varnish, and see the round circle of moisture left by my mouth on the varnish as I bent close to the desk."

In 1904 John Day accepted a newspaper job in California. While waiting for their furniture to make its way by ship around Cape Horn, the family moved into a rented house in Berkeley on San Francisco Bay. When the ship arrived, they moved a few miles south to Oakland, terminus of the transcontinental railroad and home of Idora Park, a racetrack John Day covered for his paper. Their house was surrounded by trees and flowers and had a view of the softly sloping hills to the east.

"There were hours working in the garden," Dorothy recalled, "playing with dolls made of calla leaves with roses for heads, making perfume by crushing flowers and putting them in bottles with water, playing with dirt and sand, watching anthills, gopher hills, sitting and listening to a brook, smelling geranium leaves."

Sometimes Dorothy's explorations of wildlife in Oakland were shared, and on one occasion several children joined in making tunnels through a field of thistles "looking for what we considered little rooms in those sheltered recesses among the weeds. It was like living in a green sea, a shallow sea with sunlight sifting through and the odor of the earth, and the hum of insects and the drowsy heat all around us. In one of these rooms one boy, he might have been ten or so, wanted to 'play house, mama and papa,' but this was an intrusion on my happy mind, and I rejected him."

At school she passed a note to a little boy with the simple message, "I love you." The teacher intercepted the note and kept the two after school so that she could probe "to find the wickedness that my simple words were not meant to convey. I had merely thought he was beautiful."

She kept her temper at school, but at home, if sufficiently prodded by her older brothers, she could be explosive. Her biting and kicking was supplemented by name-calling that on one occasion was so sailor-like that her mother scrubbed Dorothy's mouth out with soap. (Her temper never left her. Later in life, advised by a visitor to the Catholic Worker to speak in a more moderate way, Dorothy responded, "I hold more temper in one minute than you will hold in your entire life.")

Her childhood confessions from Oakland include the theft of a nickel from her mother's purse and the sale of a school book for ten cents. She bought candy with her stolen wealth, but once the candy was eaten, remorse drove her sorrowfully to Mother Grace to confess her wrongdoing.

On a rainy Sunday afternoon she explored the attic and came upon a musty old Bible which she spent hours reading. "I remember nothing that I read, just the sense of holiness in holding the book in my hands."

Before long, under the influence of a Methodist family next door, Dorothy had a first go at religion. "I became disgustingly, proudly pious. I sang hymns with the family next door. I prayed on my knees beside my bed. I asked my mother why we did not pray and sing hymns and got no satisfactory answer. No one went to church but me. I was alternately lonely and smug. At the same time, I began to be afraid of God, of death, of eternity. As soon as I closed my eyes at night the blackness of death surrounded me. . . . If I fell asleep God became in my ears a great noise that became louder and louder, and approached nearer and nearer to me until I woke up sweating with fear and shrieking for my mother. I fell asleep with her hand in mine, her warm presence by my bed."

Earthquake

On the evening of April 17, 1906, John Day was at the Idora Park racetrack. The weather was sultry and the horses were strangely restless, neighing and stamping in their stalls. He was struck by a sense of panic in their behavior. At 5:13 on the morning of the 18th, with a pale crescent moon hanging in the dawn sky, the bell of St. Mary's Church in Chinatown began to toll of its own accord, and was quickly joined by other bells across the city. For forty seconds the surface of the city along the San Andreas Fault rolled as if it were liquid. There were ten seconds of rest, and then a greater shock than the first that lasted twenty-five seconds. In just over a minute, an earthquake had shifted the ground under part of San Francisco twenty feet. Fires started at hundreds of locations, but the water mains had broken and little could be done to keep the blaze from spreading. The visiting opera singer, Enrico Caruso, who had sung Don José in *Carmen* the night before, woke in his bed in the Palace Hotel less in dread of death than of damage to his voice. To reassure himself, he stood at an open window of his suite and sang a passage from Umberto Giordano's *Fedora*, a performance that may have astonished some of the panicking people in the streets below even more than the earthquake. Unintentionally, he gave them courage.

Dorothy remembered waking to deep rumbling, feeling convulsions in the earth, "so that the earth became a sea which rocked our house." Water splashed from the windmill and water tank that she could see from her window. "My father took my brothers from their beds and rushed to the front door, where my mother stood with my sister, whom she had snatched from beside me. I was left in a big brass bed, which rolled back and forth on a polished floor. . . ."

Across the bay, the fires quickly became uncontrollable. Before they were extinguished, 250,000, half the city's population, were homeless, and nearly 700 were dead. Oakland was badly damaged, but was far enough off the fault line to escape devastation. "When the earth settled," Dorothy wrote, "the house was in shambles, dishes broken all over the floor, the house cracked from roof to ground. But there was no fire in Oakland." (Bret Harte said Oakland was spared "because there are some things the earth cannot swallow.")

Dorothy had dreamed of "blackness and death surrounding me" and now discovered, wide awake, that the earth was as insubstantial as it seemed in nightmares. She may have been struck by a more singular and intimate insecurity, for her family hadn't come to her rescue when the house was cracking around her. Her sister and brothers were carried outside, but she was left in her bedroom.

For two days refugees poured into Oakland by ferry and boat, emerging from San Francisco's flames and cloud bank. "Idora Park and the racetrack made camping grounds for them," Dorothy recalled. "All the neighbors joined my mother in serving the homeless. Every stitch of available clothing was given away. All day following the disaster, there were tremblings of the earth and there was fear in the air."

The worst was over and the Day family had survived without physical injury. But the plant that printed John Day's newspaper had burned, the paper was out of business, and he was out of a job. The house and much of the property that had been shipped around Cape Horn were shattered. What was still usable he sold for cash and in short order the Day family was on its way by train to Chicago, a city built on ground that behaved itself.

Chicago

The family moved into a dingy six-room tenement flat over a tavern on 37th Street. Until John Day found a job, it was all they could afford. Grace Day "had to do all her own work," Dorothy recalled, "washing for six in a large common basement which stretched almost the length of the block and was like a series of caverns where the children played on rainy days. Outside was a cement-paved yard with neither tree nor blade of grass. The nearest green was that of a vacant lot on the corner, where I wheeled my doll carriage and smelled the sweet clover, gathering sheaves of it for mother to dry in pillowcases and put in linen chests."

Lake Michigan was only two blocks away and could be seen from a window in the dining room. A breakwater had been made of slabs of limestone, and in the pools that formed behind the rock the Day brothers used to swim in the summer. Here two neighbor children drowned one sunny day. "The little boy had found himself beyond his depth and his sister . . . had taken off her dress to twist into a rope for him to catch hold of; instead he had dragged her in too and they had died in each other's arms."

Dorothy looked out over "the vast sunny lake, calm and treacherous, the weeds and grasses among the sands where little children played while older ones stood in awe close to their parents, that long quiet afternoon. When the bodies were found, we did not run to the spot, but mother hurried us home and doubtless there was panic in her heart."

It was her first real encounter with death "and yet it did not touch me nearly as those forebodings of death which came to me at night after I had closed my eyes in the dark room and the universe began to spin around me in space."

The family's sudden plunge into poverty was humiliating. Dorothy didn't want to be seen entering a tenement door and pretended to live elsewhere, sometimes passing by her own door and entering a more impressive one nearby so that school friends wouldn't see where she really lived. When Dorothy was sent shopping, she had to leave untouched the more appealing items and bring home potatoes, bread, jelly, tea and bananas—and the last only in their dead ripe condition at ten cents a dozen. And yet Grace Day managed to bring a special dignity to the household. She made curtains from remnants and hung them from fishing rods. She transformed fruit crates into bookcases, nail kegs into kitchen stools. The absence of a sewing machine did not prevent her from hand stitching the family's shirts and dresses. "All our clothes were beautifully made and laundered no matter how poor we were." Grace Day "reigned over the supper table as a queen and had as much interest in entertaining her four children as if we were adult friends at a party." Dorothy was privileged to assist in her evening bath ritual, adding a drop of cologne to the water so that its scent might briefly transform tenement living.

Grace Day had remarkable bravado which rarely cracked, though one night after supper she became hysterical and one by one broke all the dishes. Perhaps it was brought on by exhaustion and hopelessness, or came from the blinding headaches she sometimes suffered. This was a period in her life when she experienced four miscarriages. The next day she seemed her usual self.

Dorothy shared in the labor of the house. "I scoured the faucets until they shone" and had many household chores. Without knowing it, she realized later in her life, "I had imbibed 'a philosophy of work,' enjoying the creative aspects of it as well as getting satisfaction from a hard and necessary job well done."

If there was no yard, at least there was a large back porch. Here Dorothy could arrange tea parties with the dolls Grace Day had made from remnants and wooden clothespins, making faces with buttonhole mouths. It was on the porch one night, while gazing at the stars, that Mary Harrington, a Catholic neighbor four years older, told her the story of a saint. In later years Dorothy couldn't remember who it was or anything of the saint's life, only that the story filled her with enthusiasm so that her heart "almost burst with desire to take part in such high endeavor. . . . I was filled with a natural striving, a thrilling recognition of the possibilities of spiritual adventure."

Dorothy received another impulse toward Catholicism from a neighbor, Mrs. Barrett. Searching for a playmate, she discovered Mrs. Barrett praying on her knees at the side of her bed. She looked up at Dorothy without dismay or embarrassment, told her where to find her daughter, and returned to her prayer. "I felt a burst of love toward Mrs. Barrett that I have never forgotten, a feeling of gratitude and happiness that warmed my heart." For a time Dorothy prayed at bedtime and one night, while hurdy-gurdies played on the street below, she convinced Della that they should both sleep on the floor, thinking of saints sleeping on the cold stone floors of their monastic cells. She fell asleep listening to the snoring of the drunken lady who lived upstairs.

During this period of unemployment, her father labored over what he hoped would be a best-selling adventure novel, the typewriter in front of him, an ashtray on one side and a glass of whiskey on the other. The pastor of the neighborhood Episcopal church who came to visit one day, hoping to find new members for his congregation, found John Day busy with his novel. While not winning any adults to the church, he got agreement that the children could come. The two brothers joined the choir, and Dorothy listened eagerly to the music and prayers. "I loved the Psalms and the Collect prayers and learned many of them by heart, and the anthems filled me with joy. I had never heard anything so beautiful as the *Benedictus* and the *Te Deum.* The words remained with me ever since:

> All ye works of the Lord, bless ye the Lord.
> Praise Him and glorify Him forever.
> O ye sun and moon, O ye stars in the sky,
> O ye winds and hoarfrosts, ye rain and dew,
> Bless ye the Lord, praise Him and glorify Him forever.

"The song thrilled in my heart, and though I was only ten years old, through these Psalms and canticles I called on all creation to join me in blessing the Lord. I thanked Him for creating me. ...."

From her childhood, Dorothy had a marked capacity for awe and a vulnerability to beauty. "I wanted to cry out with joy. ... I always felt the common unity of all humanity; the longing of the human heart is for this communion. If only I could sing, I thought, I would shout before the Lord, and call upon the world to shout with me, 'All ye works of the Lord, bless ye the Lord, praise Him and glorify Him forever.' "

Webster Avenue

At last John Day found work—appointment as sports editor of *The Inter Ocean*. The Day family moved, first to Oakwood Boulevard and then to a large house near Lincoln Park on Webster Avenue on Chicago's North Side. Here there was privacy for all, a bedroom fireplace for Grace Day and, great treasure, a library, in the center of which was a "large round table with a green cover and a lamp in the middle, a gas lamp, green shaded, with a long green hose that always smelled slightly of gas." The chairs were arranged so that all could read by the same light.

Dorothy loved words, rejoiced in the way they could be sewn together to change seasons, leap across time and space, or simply describe the ordinary things around her that she found most captivating. By the age of ten she had become a passionate reader. Sitting with her back to the gas lamp in the library of the Webster Avenue house, she read Victor Hugo, Charles Dickens, Robert Louis Stevenson, James Fenimore Cooper and Edgar Allan Poe. Here she first read *The Imitation of Christ* by Thomas à Kempis, though she also liked books that her father banned as "trash." Romances that Dorothy borrowed from friends at school were not to be read in the library or anywhere where John Day might notice them. The "dime novels" that her brother preferred had similarly to be kept out of sight. "I can remember one with a lurid cover of ten robed and hooded men walking in single file along a mountain path with a boa constrictor gliding along behind them." Dorothy hid Swinburne's poem, *Tristram*, with its pictures of lovers lying in the grass, behind a bookcase.

The Day daughters weren't allowed out of the house without permission. "The fact that father kept us from going out, and did not want company to come in, saved us from the busy existence that most persons had," she recalled with a remarkable lack of annoyance. In fact, books weren't full-time companions, and life wasn't simply to be read about. She could recall "sad summer afternoons when there was nothing to do, and suddenly everything palled and life was dull and uninteresting." But on Sundays, at least, there was worship at the Episcopal church and during the warmer months there were Sunday afternoon band concerts at Lincoln Park, where large crowds of picnickers gathered. Dorothy fell briefly but madly in love with the band's violinist and shuddered if he happened to glance at her.

"We never exchanged a word but I hungered for his look."

Dorothy turned fifteen in 1912, and in May of that year the last of the Day children was born, a baby brother named John who was often put in Dorothy's care. Before 2 A.M., when John Day returned from his newspaper job, the baby was brought to Dorothy's bed, where she was expected to keep him from crying so that her father's sleep wouldn't be disturbed. Every night Dorothy had to rock him to sleep, singing from the Episcopal hymnal until her back and shoulders ached. "But the very hardship of taking care of him, the hours I put in with him, made me love him all the more."

Before dawn, with John changed, fed, and sleeping, Dorothy could turn to her homework, especially Latin and Greek, history (which she found dull) and English composition. The ancient languages delighted her. She was one of several students who had an extra voluntary class in Greek and Latin after school. For ten cents she bought a second-hand copy of the Greek New Testament and wrote her own translation.

While her experiment at sleeping monk-like on the floor was a one-night event, Dorothy continued to be fascinated with piety. In her journal she declared what "poor weak creatures we are" and what hard work it is to overcome temptation. "I am working always, always on guard, praying without ceasing to overcome all physical sensations and be purely spiritual . . . the only love is of God and is spiritual without taint of earthliness. I am afraid I have never really experienced this love or I would never crave the sensual love or the thrill that comes with the meeting of lips. . . . Oh, surely it is a continual strife and my spirit is weary."

If the writing was painfully adolescent, the subject was in fact one that she never lost interest in: the apparent conflict of flesh and the spirit. In fact, the only "meeting of lips" she had yet personally experienced, she admitted, was "a firm, austere kiss from my mother every night."

In her last year at high school, radical political sensitivities began to take root. Her oldest brother Donald got his first newspaper job with *The Day Book* (no connection to the Day family). The journal carried no advertisements and thus could expose working conditions in factories and department stores without fear of lost revenue. In *The Day Book*, Dorothy first became aware of the American labor movement and the Left—the Socialist Party led by Eugene Debs, and the Industrial Workers of the World.

Dorothy's reading took a sharp turn to the left. She read not only Jack London's adventurous novels but his essays on the class struggle. In Peter Kropotkin, she discovered a scientist who had renounced his aristocratic origins and become a "revolutionist." His vision of an anarchist social order based on cooperation rather than competition had a lifelong meaning to her, and into old age she often recommended some of his books: *The Memoirs of a Revolutionist*, *Mutual Aid*, *The Conquest of Bread*, and *Fields, Factories and Workshops.* Kropotkin, she said, "brought to my mind the plight of the poor."

It was Upton Sinclair, however, that took Dorothy away from the library and bandstand in the park and made her return to those areas of urban poverty in which she had earlier lived in such shame. She came upon his novel, *The Jungle*, which was set in and around Chicago's vast stockyards and slaughterhouses. The chief character, Jurgis Rudkus, a Lithuanian immigrant, was the only member of his family not utterly destroyed by squalor and injustice. Finally he committed himself to struggle for a just social order by joining the Socialist Party. The novel's depiction of filth and violence in the meat industry so shocked its readers that the book is given credit for Congressional passage of tough meat-inspection laws, although Sinclair had hoped to stimulate more profound social change. "I aimed at the public's heart," he commented, "and by accident hit it in the stomach."

He did reach Dorothy's heart. She began taking long walks toward the grim West Side of Chicago rather than along the lake or in the green of Lincoln Park. "I walked for miles, pushing my brother in his carriage," exploring "interminable grey streets, fascinating in their dreary sameness, past tavern after tavern, where I envisioned such scenes as the Polish wedding party in Sinclair's story."

She found a kind of beauty in the midst of destitution. "There were tiny flower gardens and vegetable patches in the yards. Often there were rows of corn, stunted but still recognizable, a few tomato plants, and always the vegetables were bordered by flowers, often grateful marigolds, all sizes and shades with their pungent odor." The drab streets seemed to be saved by pungent odors: "The odor of geranium leaves, tomato plants, marigolds; the smell of lumber, of tar, of roasting coffee; the smell of good bread and rolls and coffee cake coming from the small German bakeries. Here was enough beauty to satisfy me." Her view was no longer that of so many people she knew who regarded the poor as shiftless and worthless and whose sufferings were no one's fault but their own. Walking such streets as a fifteen-year-old, she pondered the poor and the workers and felt "that from then on my life was to be linked to theirs, their interests were to be mine: I had received a call, a vocation, a direction in my life."

That direction in life no longer drew her toward church services. The church's way of responding to injustice and poverty, she realized, was to be kind to the poor but not to open its doors to them. If it shed occasional tears for their tragedies, it did not raise a cry against those who piled up fortunes at their expense. Rather, "the rich were smiled at and fawned upon by churchgoers." Dorothy didn't "see anyone taking off his coat and giving it to the poor. I didn't see anyone having a banquet and calling in the lame, the halt and the blind."

University

In 1914, with Charlie Chaplin's baggy-trousered tramp first on the screen and world war breaking out in Europe, Dorothy, then sixteen years old, graduated from Waller High School. Thanks to her Latin and Greek, she had done well enough to be one of three students at Waller to win a scholarship. This not only made college possible but offered her the welcome prospect of being some distance from her father's irritation with foreigners, agitators, radicals and trashy books. In September, "filled with a great sense of independence," she took the two-hour train ride south to the University of Illinois campus at Urbana. She had no idea what she wanted to do with her life. Though signed up to study Latin, English, history, biology and rhetoric, in fact she felt no special interest in a particular course of studies or in gaining a degree. The main thing was that "I was on my own, and no longer to be cared for by the family. The idea of earning my own living, by my own work, was more thrilling than the idea of an education."

At college Dorothy made no attempt to join a sorority or to obtain a campus job and settle into student housing. "While I was free to go to college, I was mindful of girls who worked in stores and factories through their youth and afterward married men who were slaves in those same factories. The Marxist slogan, 'Workers of the world, unite! You have nothing to lose but your chains,' seemed to me a most stirring battle cry ... a clarion call that made me feel one with the masses [and] apart from the bourgeoisie, the smug, and the satisfied."

Choosing strenuous physical labor as her means of support, she found a succession of domestic jobs doing washing and ironing and child care in trade for bed and board. "Many a time I scrubbed the skin off my knuckles." She earned small amounts writing for the local paper. Little support came from home, as John Day's paper had folded and he was again unemployed. What money she had was largely spent on books. The words of the sixteenth-century scholar Erasmus of Rotterdam could have been her own: "When I get a little money I buy books, and if anything is left over I buy food and clothes." In her own case it was food and cigarettes, the latter a newly acquired taste.

Kropotkin had stirred her interest in Russian authors and now she discovered several others whom she would read year after year into the last week of her life: Gorki, Chekhov, Tolstoy, and, most important of all, Dostoyevsky. The last two provided a thread of connection with a religious faith that she was otherwise militantly shrugging off, feeling that "religion would only impede my work."

Classes were far less interesting to her than reading. "Really, I led a very shiftless life, doing for the first time exactly what I wanted to do, attending only those classes I wished to attend, coming and going at whatever hour of the night I pleased. My freedom intoxicated me. I felt it was worth going hungry for."

She joined a writers' club, the Scribblers, which accepted her on the basis of an essay on the experience of hunger, in which "with grim relish" she described going for three days on no food other than salted peanuts while living in a frigid attic room that contained a bed, table, chair and tiny stove which in those few days was of no use.

Dorothy read the history of the labor movement and became familiar with the speeches and writings of Big Bill Haywood, Mother Jones, Elizabeth Gurley Flynn, Eugene Debs, Carlo Tresca, and the Haymarket anarchists (labor organizers, four of whom were hanged in 1887 after being tried in Chicago).

It disturbed her that so much more was done to assist the victims of social evils than to get rid of those evils in the first place. "There were day nurseries for children . . . but why didn't fathers get money enough to take care of their families so that mothers would not have to work?" She was haunted by her awareness of the world's castoff people: "Disabled men, without arms and legs, blind men, consumptive men with all their manhood drained out of them by industrialism; farmers gaunt and harried with debt; mothers weighed down with children at their skirts, in their arms, in their wombs; people ailing and rickety—all this long procession of desperate people called to me. Where were the saints to try to change the social order, not just to minister to the slaves but to do away with slavery?"

Her heroes were those who at great risk and sacrifice were building up unions and cooperatives and struggling for the eight-hour day. In 1915, the ten-hour workday was common, and only eight percent of America's workers were union members. Many had died or been crippled to win each percentage point. "My heart thrilled at those unknown women in New England," Dorothy wrote, "who led the first strike to liberate women and children from the cotton mills." She was grateful that her mother's heart was touched by such events as well. Grace Day told Dorothy of a period in her own childhood when her family's poverty was such that she had been forced to work in a Poughkeepsie shirt factory.

Dorothy took the step of joining the Socialist Party and met with Urbana's small group of members, but she found the meetings dull and her involvement as a dues-paying member was short-lived.

Dorothy ignored much of the college's social life, but friendships slowly developed with two other students, Samson Raphaelson and Rayna Simons. Raphaelson was a gifted writer and satirist who eventually became an immensely successful playwright, and the scriptwriter for a succession of Hollywood's better comedies as well as the first "talkie," *The Jazz Singer*. But the more important friendship for Dorothy was with Rayna, three years older than herself, "slight and bony, deliciously awkward and yet unself-conscious, alive and eager." She had a mass of curly red hair, "loose enough about her face to form an aureole, a flaming aureole, with sun and brightness in it. Whatever she did, she did with her whole heart." The fact that she was Jewish meant that, despite family wealth, personal warmth and brilliance as a student, Rayna was invited into no sorority. Through Rayna, Dorothy had her first experience of anti-Semitism.

Their friendship was "clear as a bell, crystal clear, with no stain of self-seeking." The two became inseparable. During the summer, Dorothy stayed on a farm owned by Rayna's father, and in the fall she accepted Rayna's invitation to share her room in an Urbana boarding house for Jewish girls. Together they attended concerts, heard lectures on socialism and feminism, and listened to Edgar Lee Masters, Vachel Lindsay and John Masefield read their own poetry.

Rayna was loved by many, Dorothy wrote in *The Long Loneliness*, "because she was so unself-conscious, so interested in others, so ready to hear and discuss all that interested them." While still at the university, Rayna's selfless love of people had not yet drawn her toward any political ideology. She didn't share Dorothy's radical views. Dorothy found Rayna too intellectual. (Not many years later, Rayna's thinking turned as red as her hair. In 1927, while Americans were waiting in long lines to see *The Jazz Singer*, Rayna was in Moscow to take part in the massive celebration of the tenth anniversary of the Russian Revolution. While there she made arrangements to enter the Lenin Institute, a graduate school for revolutionists, but in mid-November she fell ill, and a week later she died. The next morning her body was carried by mourners to Moscow's New Crematorium. The journalist Vincent Sheean was among those weeping. "The bier was draped in the red flag and covered with golden flowers," he wrote in *Personal History*. "Then a signal was given, a switch was turned, and the golden mass of Rayna, her hair and her bright flowers and the Red flag, sank slowly before us into the furnace.")

Radical Reporter

In June 1916, Dorothy decided that she had had enough of the classroom and joined her parents in moving to New York where John Day had been hired by *The New York Telegraph*. Dorothy, now eighteen, found it easy to be with her mother again as well as with Della and four-year-old John, but she found sharing a house with her father more difficult than ever. Neither hesitated to annoy the other with contrary opinions. Dorothy decided that she needed an apartment of her own, and a job. She began searching for employment as a reporter.

With a portfolio of her clippings from Urbana, she set out applying at various New York daily papers. Quickly she found that she was lucky to get past the office boys. The only two city editors she managed to talk with assured her that urban reporting was definitely not for girls, a view shared by John Day. One editor gave her the address of a rural newspaper he thought she might try. But Dorothy was determined to stay in New York and persisted with her search, despite a deep anguish she felt, and that condition of spirit she later called "the long loneliness."

"In all that city of seven millions, I found no friends; I had no work; I was separated from my fellows. Silence in the midst of the city noises oppressed me. My own silence, the feeling that I had no one to talk to, overwhelmed me so that my very throat was constricted; my heart was heavy with unuttered thoughts; I wanted to weep my loneliness away."

The weeks of futile job-hunting at least made her intimate with New York. Each day she walked the streets and discovered the autonomous ethnic communities that were packed side by side like squares in a patch-work quilt. She became familiar with the bus and subway routes and the several bridges "that were strung like jewels over the East River."

New York's poverty was more appalling than Chicago's. Homeless and jobless men haunted the streets. The loud clatter of the "El"—the elevated trains—and the subways jarred her nerves. The rotting tenements shed a "smell like no other in the world and one never can become accustomed to it. . . . It is not the smell of life, but the smell of the grave."

And yet she found her burden of loneliness was eased when she walked through the slums.

It took five months before she arrived at the place where, given her

17

politics, she might have first applied: the offices of New York's one Socialist daily, *The Call*, down on Pearl Street, near the Brooklyn Bridge in lower Manhattan. A small and struggling paper with office space over a printing plant, here there was no one to ward off visitors who wanted to talk to the city editor. A copy boy rushing downstairs to the press room ignored her. There were a few men busy at their typewriters and several others reading copy at another desk. She introduced herself to the editor and asked him for a job. Chester Wright had no objection to women journalists, nor did he mind that she was young and new to reporting. The problem was, he told her, that *The Call* hadn't enough money to hire her. "Why, we hardly have enough money to pay the office boy!"

"That's all right," she assured him. "I wasn't expecting a big salary." She argued that the paper needed a woman reporter on the staff; there were people who might talk more easily to a woman than a man, and doors she might get through that men would find locked.

"I know, women reporters are always a good thing," Wright agreed, "but we're broke, simply broke."

While showing him her portfolio, Dorothy had an inspiration. She remembered there were some city policemen who had organized themselves into "diet squads" in order to demonstrate that the poor could live well enough on $5 a week. Some wealthy women in Chicago were feeding themselves on a quarter a day. If *The Call* would pay her just $5 a week—what a lot of factory girls were getting, she pointed out—she could be a "diet squad of one" and write from a more radical perspective about the experience for *The Call*.

Perhaps the idea appealed to Chester Wright, or perhaps he had developed admiration for the sheer bravado of this eager, ambitious, attractive young woman. He agreed to hire her for a month at $5 a week, and if he decided to keep her, somehow he would find the money to pay her $12 a week afterward.

The next morning Dorothy packed her suitcase, said goodbye to her parents, left the suitcase at *The Call*, and went out in search of her own lodging. On Cherry Street there were many tenements displaying "furnished room" signs and in one of them she easily found something that seemed suitable. Rent was $5 a month. There were vermin in the mattress, she found out during the first night, and the loose panes in her window rattled with the steady draft from the narrow air shaft beyond. With the draft came the stench from the hall toilets. At night the neighborhood cats "shrieked with almost human voices." Even so, Dorothy was delighted with what she had found and felt that she had been led to her new home by a guardian angel.

Having a room and a job, her sense of isolation evaporated. The staff of *The Call* quickly absorbed Dorothy into their social life, inviting her to join them at Child's Restaurant on Park Row in the small hours of the night after the day's edition had gone to press. Here they renewed their permanent arguments about their competing radical ideologies. Some of the staff favored the anarchist "Wobblies" who were attempting to gather all workers, whether skilled or unskilled, into one vast union. The Wobbly heroes included Big Bill Haywood and Joe Hill, the labor organizer who had been executed by a firing squad in Utah but whose songs were heard on every picket line. Others aligned themselves with the American Federation of Labor, whose membership was restricted to skilled industrial workers, the elite of labor, who took a longer and less revolutionary view of change than Wobblies. There were other factions as well, though as yet there was no Communist Party. Socialism, in its variety, was well represented by *The Call*'s staff. Dorothy took no sides.

Her new neighborhood seemed more interesting than any political theory. "It was a cheerful and lively street with horse carts which jogged every half hour through the crowds of children playing in the gutters and hiding among ash cans. The air was full of shrill child voices, shouted admonitions from the mothers hanging over their fire-escapes which fronted the buildings like grim skeletons. Street organs surrounded by little girls played the latest popular tunes and every once in a while a merry-go-round set on a wagon was drawn to the curb by a lean and deafened horse. Rides were a penny and the music which the man ground out as he turned the handle which set the carousel spinning held an invitation which gathered the children from blocks around."

Nearby was Mulberry Street with its Greek and Turkish coffee shops and "shops where long cheeses and sausages and chains of red pepper and garlic contributed their smell to the cluttered air."

But streets that seemed almost heavenly in the day turned sinister late at night, when Dorothy made her way home. The noise of her footsteps so disturbed the silence that she bought rubber heels for her shoes. People were rarely to be seen, but she discovered she wasn't alone. "A whole silent world was alive, a world that slept at dawn. . . . There were huge sleek cats, furtive pariahs that prowled through the hallways and gutters."

Yet even the night world revealed its delights, such as the bakeries filling the darkness with the smell of bread in the ovens. A small tobacco shop gleamed brightly on one corner, a harbor of warmth.

The night had its own population. One of them was a woman who ran along the streets calling out the name of a long dead son. One winter night, when Dorothy stopped to talk with two policemen who had built a small fire in a shelter under the Manhattan Bridge and were having a midnight meal of coffee and rolls, the woman came running down the street. The policemen welcomed her.

"How about it, mother. You haven't found him yet? Better come and get warm and have a cup of coffee. You've hunted long enough tonight."

The woman's name was Audrey, and despite her age and her beaten face she was able to make a slight living as a prostitute. She was known locally as "Dis-audrey conduct," in recognition of the charge under which she was often arrested.

From such adventures Dorothy returned to her tiny room, with its bed, table and chair and small library. She had decorated the dingy walls with pictures of a bullfighter, a famous explorer, and a postcard of a bust of Amenemhat III, the Egyptian king of thirty-seven centuries earlier, a handsome image despite a blow to the stone that had cost it part of the nose. Dorothy in fact liked "the desolate line of his broken nose, and the pleasant sensuousness of his expression." There was a record player as well. By limiting her food budget to twenty-five cents a day, she would be able to pay a dollar a week for this mechanical roommate. Grace Day contributed fifteen records.

Dorothy wrote up her diet, the purchase of record player and other details of her life in a series of four articles for *The Call*, one of which ran under the headline, REPORTER EATS FARINA AND CHEESE AND READS WORDSWORTH.

Red Friends, Revolutionary News

If the first month's diet was meager, Dorothy's work provided well for her huge appetite for experience. "There was much to do—meetings to attend of protest against labor, capital, the high cost of living, war-profiteering, entering the war, not entering the war, conscription, anti-conscription. There were meetings to start strikes, to end strikes, to form unions, to fight against unions. Food riots came. . . . There were birth control meetings—trials of birth control leaders . . . and interviews galore."

At one demonstration Dorothy was clubbed by a policeman. She was surprised at how easily she had herself been caught up in "the spirit of the mob." When the club struck her ribs with a hollow thud, she was in such a state that it didn't hurt nor did it even anger her. All she felt was a "curious, detached, mad feeling . . . as the crowd seethed and shouted and fought." She looked at the policeman whose club had struck her and noticed blood flowing from a gash in his forehead. He wiped the blood from his eyes and was distressed to see he had hit a young woman wearing a press card. "Excuse me," he said. "I can't see." He then renewed his use of the club on others in the howling crowd. It happened it wasn't a radical crowd that day but flag-waving youth demonstrating for America to join the war in Europe.

Dorothy was sent up to East 15th Street to write about a shelter for probationers, which turned out to be a warm, caring house of hospitality to which judges occasionally sent women—often young prostitutes—who might otherwise have gone to prison. Miss Prince, the house's founder and fund-raiser, spoke with Dorothy of her hope that someday there might be enough such houses so that prisons would no longer be needed.

One night in 1917, Dorothy covered a speech by Elizabeth Gurley Flynn, who later in her life went to prison for her leadership of the American Communist Party. However in 1917 there was as yet no Communist Party. Flynn was a Wobbly, and that night she was in New York to raise financial help for iron miners on strike in Mesabi, Minnesota. Many in the audience, including Dorothy, wept as Flynn described the violence that was being heaped upon the strikers, the appalling conditions of the mines, and the destitution being suffered by the miners' families. When a collection was taken up for them, Dorothy emptied her purse, "not even saving carfare, so that I had to borrow the fare back to the office and go without lunch for some days afterward."

Dorothy was assigned to interview Leon Trotsky who was living in exile in an apartment on St. Mark's Place on the Lower East Side. Soon after the interview, he was back in Russia where he became one of the dominant figures of the November Revolution and a founder of the Soviet state. Little of Dorothy's interview was published in *The Call*, however, as the editors didn't welcome Trotsky's belief that the American Socialist Party was naive.

The 1917 revolution in Russia, hardly a naive event, came in two stages. In March, faced by strikers and an army that ignored his orders, the Tsar yielded to both liberal and radical pressure and abdicated, and a provisional government was established. The worker Soviets (the Russian word for council) were not yet in power, but a thousand-year monarchy had collapsed. That event produced jubilation among radicals throughout the world. On March 21, Dorothy was among the many thousands in New York's Madison Square Garden. "I felt the exultation, the joyous sense of the victory of the masses as they sang . . . the workers' hymn of Russia:

> Arise, ye prisoners of starvation!
> Arise, ye wretched of the earth!
> For justice thunders condemnation,
> A better world's in birth.
> No more tradition's chains shall bind us,
> No more enslaved, no more enthralled,
> The earth shall rise on new foundations.
> We have been naught, we shall be all.
> 'Tis the final conflict,
> Let each stand in his place . . .
> The international working class
> Shall be the human race.

It was a festival of hope. Heaven was descending to earth.

Among those singing the "Internationale" with Dorothy that night was Mike Gold, a co-worker at *The Call* who had already become a close friend. He had been born on the Lower East Side of an Orthodox Jewish family and had "no politics except hunger" until 1914, when he strayed into a demonstration at Union Square and was knocked down by the police when they attacked the demonstrators. By the end of the day he had bought a copy of *The Masses*, the Socialist monthly magazine, and began to gravitate into the Socialist Party. His book *Jews Without Money*, published in 1930, remains a classic novel of the urban poor. When the Communist Party was founded in the United States after the November Revolution in Russia, he became a member and later in his life was editor of the Communist paper, *The Daily Worker*.

He was twenty-three years old when Dorothy met him. He, too, had joined the paper's staff when he was eighteen. After midnight, when *The Call* had been turned over to the printers, they were among the reporters who went to Child's for pancakes and coffee. During a period when she was sick, it was he who came after work one day to bring her cough medicine, lemons and some whiskey, as well as an essay on Maxim Gorki, a Russian writer they both liked. The landlady came to her own conclusions about why Mike Gold was in Dorothy's room and called Grace Day to notify her of Dorothy's immoral conduct. Grace Day quickly came to visit and accepted Dorothy's reassurance that she and Mike were friends, not lovers.

It is not surprising that gossip about them continued to be plentiful. The two spent long hours walking the streets, sitting on piers along the waterfront on the East River, talking about life and sharing experiences about the passion that had brought them both to *The Call*—the sufferings of the poor. They both loved books and rejoiced to talk about their reading. Sometimes Mike broke into song—whether in Hebrew or Yiddish, Dorothy didn't know.

Another lifelong friendship that began in 1917 was with Peggy Baird, whom Dorothy met through Mike Gold. Peggy was an artist who lived in a large, wildly unkempt room and who was baffled at Dorothy's seeming immunity to sexual temptation. Peggy rejoiced to find lovers. She assured Dorothy that sex was "a barrier that kept men and women from fully understanding each other, and thus a barrier to be broken down." Love affairs, she said, were "incidents in an erotic education." Dorothy neither agreed nor disagreed, but was fascinated with Peggy's openness and sense of adventure. The fact that Peggy "sexed," as she called it, and Dorothy didn't wasn't a barrier between them. Peggy recruited Dorothy as a model. "Just strip off your clothes," she said to Dorothy after coffee was brewed one morning. "The room's warm enough. And while you're drinking your coffee, I'll sketch you." It struck Dorothy that she wouldn't dream of undressing before her mother or sister, and yet it was impossible to refuse Peggy's request. She slipped out of her clothes, curled up on the sofa, and comforted herself with a cigarette. "You'll probably have a beautiful figure by the time you're thirty," Peggy said reassuringly.

(Half a century later, Peggy settled at the Catholic Worker farm, and while there was received into the Catholic Church. Even when she was slowly dying of cancer, people were drawn to her just as they had been when she was a young woman in Greenwich Village. "It is wonderful," Dorothy wrote in her journal during Peggy's last months," how young and old turn to Peggy, who is always calm, equable, unjudging. She has something. . . .")

The Masses

Dorothy's work experiences at *The Call* came so thick and fast that she found it impossible to piece them together in a coherent way. "Life on a newspaper," she wrote, "whether radical or conservative, made me lose all sense of perspective. ... I was carried along in a world of events, writing, reporting, with no time at all for thought or reflection, one day listening to Trotsky, and the next day interviewing Mrs. Vincent Astor's butler. ... " The emerging pattern of Dorothy's life, with its fierce intellectual and spiritual needs, required more space for reflection than was possible on a daily paper.

Her last *Call* assignment brought her to Washington where, on April 2, 1917, President Wilson addressed both houses of Congress and war was declared. On her return, she went to Webster Hall in lower Manhattan to attend a dance which had been organized to raise money for a group of anarchists who were opposing the draft. One anarchist approached Dorothy so aggressively that she slapped him. He slapped her back. Others intervened on behalf of Dorothy and roughly ushered the anarchist out. Mike Gold had watched it all, was critical of Dorothy's part in the event, and told her so. She responded by resigning her job and walking out. Her stay with *The Call* had lasted seven months.

For several weeks she worked with the Anti-Conscription League until late in the month when she joined the staff of *The Masses*, the monthly magazine whose staff and contributors were the aristocracy of America's left. Max Eastman, the editor, was a poet and speaker who, in the early years following the Russian Revolution, was one of its most uncritical admirers, but who later became a disillusioned and bitter anti-Communist and an editor of *Reader's Digest*. Floyd Dell, who hired Dorothy, had quit high school at sixteen, worked in a factory, become a Chicago journalist, made a name as a poet, and finally started writing for *The Masses*. Later he was best known as a novelist. John Reed, after graduating from Harvard, was a combination labor organizer and radical reporter. A friend of Lenin's, his eye-witness account of the Russian Revolution was published as *Ten Days That Shook the World*. In 1919, at the age of thirty-two, he was a founder of the American Communist Labor Party. A year later he died in

Moscow. Honored as a hero of the Revolution, his ashes were buried by the Kremlin wall.

The offices of *The Masses*, appropriately, looked out over Union Square. The walls were decorated with original drawings and cartoons by the leading artists of the Left: Art Young, Hugo Gellert, Boardman Robinson, Maurice Becker, Henry Glintencamp and others. Delivering new work, the artists often paused for conversation and coffee away from the drawing board. The magazine's poets were often there as well, and on occasion there were spontaneous poetry readings.

The government took *The Masses* seriously. "Max Eastman," Dorothy recalled, "was carrying on a scholarly controversy with President Wilson: the letters they exchanged were printed monthly in the magazine which I helped to dummy up at a printer's on Park Row with Floyd Dell, who patiently taught me how to be an editor along these mechanical lines."

Her main work was to sort through the many submissions the magazine received and to decide which ones should be seen by the senior editors. It was meditative, quiet work, in contrast to reporting for a daily, and gave her a chance to think more and gain perspective.

Her rift with Mike Gold was short-lived. They read Tolstoy together, renewed their explorations of the slums and waterfront, and together welcomed red-haired Rayna when she came visiting from Chicago. "In our radical ardor we made friends with the world; many a time, coming home late at night, we picked up men from the park benches and gave them whatever bed was empty in the place, ourselves sitting up all night, continuing to talk." Together they went to visit the younger brother of artist Hugo Gellert, held in a military prison for his refusal to wear a uniform or take part in the war. There was at the time no legal provision for conscientious objectors. Despite everything, the boy was cheerful; he had been allowed to keep his violin. But a few weeks later he was dead, officially a suicide. Those who knew him couldn't believe it, and Hugo Gellert took for granted his brother had been murdered. "I could see the blind greed of the industrialist," Dorothy wrote, "but the cold, calculating torture and killing of prisoners was a mystery that left me shuddering."

Repression wasn't only for young men who refused to kill. It came in milder forms to those who opposed the war with words and symbolic gestures. Each issue of *The Masses* was studied by the postal authorities before being accepted for delivery. One was refused because of a poem about Mary, the mother of Jesus, having become pregnant out of wedlock. Another was judged undeliverable on the grounds that it contained pornography — there was a drawing in it of a nude woman. An issue that offered prizes to winners of an essay contest was refused because the contest was deemed a lottery.

The harassment of the magazine, however, generated news and, despite Post Office suppression, circulation managed to climb steadily. In September federal officers raided the magazine and seized back issues, manuscripts, financial records, subscriber lists and all the files of correspondence. The Post Office rescinded the magazine's mailing permit. Five of the editors and two leading contributors were indicted on the charge of sedition.

Dorothy's name was new to the magazine's masthead. She wasn't arrested and managed to get out the last issue of *The Masses*, dated November-December 1917, which included her own lyrical description of Manhattan's South Street, "where truckmen and dockmen sit around on loads of boxes and wait for a boat to come in, where men idle in the September sunlight and dream and yawn and smoke . . . where kids sit on the edge of the dock and look with wistful eyes at the water below that swirls with refuse and driftwood."

Jail

In the spring of 1917 pacifists had been demonstrating in Washington, but the suffragists had been picketing at the White House all year protesting the exclusion of women from the voting booth and public office. Among those arrested and jailed for thirty days was Peggy Baird. On her release in November, she briefly returned to New York, met Dorothy and Mike Gold in a basement cafe in Greenwich Village, and described "the stir" the imprisoned women were making. "I wouldn't use the vote if I had it," Peggy said, "but that doesn't keep me from joining them when they're making such a good fight." She planned to return to Washington the next day and wondered if Dorothy would like to take part in the next series of actions, now that *The Masses* had been suppressed. A number of women planned to get arrested in front of the White House and would fast once in jail to protest the treatment to which suffragists were being subjected.

"I don't see why I shouldn't go," Dorothy responded. "I hate not to be working and I don't see what else there is I can do right now." Mike took them to the terminal to catch the night bus.

The next day, November 10, a procession of nearly forty women formed at Lafayette Park, across the street from the White House. With banners in hand, each wearing a purple and gold silk sash, they walked two by two like cathedral choristers toward the White House gates. "There was a religious flavor about the silent proceeding," Dorothy wrote, "and a holy light shone on the faces of the suffragists." A crowd stood by watching. "There were old women who cheered, young women whose faces glowed or were apathetic. Men were generally indignant, except the newspaper reporters, and they were enthusiastic because the suffragists were providing them with so many good stories. Some men shouted, 'Shame! In wartime too!' " Jeering boys threw stones while sailors and soldiers were attempting to seize the women's banners.

Arrest quickly followed, but not jail. The judge who faced the feminists found them guilty but postponed sentence. The women marched back to the White House, repeated their action, were arrested again, and the next morning won their sentences: six months for the leader of the action, fifteen days for the oldest defendant, and thirty days for the rest. Immediately, they declared themselves hunger strikers, refusing to eat until imprisoned

27

suffragists were treated not as criminals but were granted the privileges given to political prisoners in Europe: use of their own clothes, passage of letters without censorship, access to their own doctors and lawyers, and possession of books and personal papers.

It all seemed like a marvelous adventure to Dorothy until she was on the train under police escort, watching in melancholy the lamps glowing in farmhouse windows on the way to Occoquan, a penal workhouse rumored to treat prisoners brutally. "Somehow," she told Peggy, "life and struggle seem very tawdry in the twilight. This bleak countryside makes me feel that I should struggle for my soul instead of political rights. . . . I feel peculiarly small and lonely tonight."

At the workhouse the male guards, two to each woman, seized the prisoners. The eldest was picked off the floor. Dorothy managed to bite the hand of the warden and then plant solid kicks in the shins of the guards who carried her off. "I struggled every step of the way." Finally the guards lifted her up and threw her onto an iron bench, one of them yelling, "My mother ain't no suffrager!" Dorothy was locked in a cell with another prisoner who had been notably rowdy and had been handcuffed to the bars in punishment. The two went to sleep talking quietly of the novels of Joseph Conrad and of travel and the spell of the sea.

By the third day of the hunger strike, Dorothy was suffering deep depression. She watched the light slowly shifting in her cell and experienced "a heart-breaking conviction of the ugliness of life." She had no feeling of her own identity, no sense of future possibilities. How must it be, she wondered, for those imprisoned not merely for weeks but years? She had heard of women kept for up to half a year in solitary confinement cells, and prisoners talked of a whipping post for those who weren't otherwise subdued. And here she was "with thirty-seven other women—all in order that the papers might give the cause publicity and make the public think about suffrage." She wondered what good would suffrage do if it were won. No doubt many suffragists would vote for war just as men did. "I lost all consciousness of any cause. . . . I could only feel darkness and desolation all around me.

"That I would be free again after thirty days meant nothing to me. I would never be free again, never free when I knew that behind bars all over the world there are women and men, young girls and boys, suffering constraint, punishment, isolation and hardship for crimes of which all of us are guilty. . . . People sold themselves for jobs, for the pay check, and if they received a high enough price, they were honored. If their cheating, their theft, their lie, were of colossal proportions, if it were successful, they met with praise, not blame."

More than ever before, Dorothy felt a profound sense of identification with those whom most people view with horror and in whom they see no glimpse of themselves: "I was the mother whose child had been raped and slain. I was the mother who had borne the monster who had done it. I was even that monster, feeling in my own breast every abomination."

Her sleep was broken by nightmares, and in the days she ached with dull hunger.

She asked for a Bible and two days later it was given to her. It was only for literary enjoyment, she assured herself. But as she turned to the Psalms, which she had first loved in her childhood, more than ever before they became a source of joy:

> They that sow in tears shall reap in joy.
> Going, they went and wept, casting their seeds.
> But coming, they shall come with joyfulness, carrying their
>   sheaves.

"If we had faith in what we were doing," she realized freshly, "making our protest against brutality and injustice, then we were indeed casting our seeds, and there was the promise of the harvest to come."

At the end of the sixth day of the hunger strike, the women were transferred to the prison hospital. On the eighth day, Dorothy could go on no further, accepted a crust of bread soaked in milk, but then resumed the fast. On the tenth day the fasters' demands were suddenly met, the women were given back their own clothes, presented with all the mail that had accumulated, given liberty to walk the jail corridors, and served delicious meals. When they had their strength back, they were transferred to the Washington City Jail where they were allowed to pick their own cells and do as they pleased, as if they were guests rather than convicts. Then on November 28 came the astonishing news that they were free at President Wilson's own order. The warden was jubilant: "A pardon signed by the President! Now you'll be home to eat Thanksgiving dinners."

"We don't want a pardon," one of the women responded. "We have committed no crime to be pardoned for."

"All the same," the warden said, "out you go!"

The Golden Swan

The Golden Swan, a saloon at 6th Avenue and 4th Street in Greenwich Village, was a place of refuge for a number of writers and radicals of the day including Eugene O'Neill, playwright of the nearby Provincetown Playhouse. Despite the burst of recognition that had come in 1916 with the opening of his first play, *Bound East for Cardiff*, O'Neill was depressed and drinking heavily in the winter of 1917. His affair with Louise Bryant had recently ended with her departure for Moscow where she joined John Reed and wrote about the Russian Revolution. When Dorothy returned to New York from her ordeal in Washington, she met O'Neill at The Golden Swan. Friendship struck up between the two so readily that it seemed to his friends that Dorothy might fill the space left by Bryant. Though O'Neill was nine years older, the two had made some similar choices: both had dropped out of college; both had become reporters; both were attempting to make their living as writers; both were drawn to outcasts.

They also had in common an itchy, hesitantly confessed awareness of the presence of God. Agnes Boulton, who was then sharing a Village apartment with Dorothy and who later married O'Neill, quickly realized that Dorothy was subject to "sudden and unexplainable impulses" which drew her "into any nearby Catholic church"—a religious longing similar to O'Neill's.

Agnes Boulton recalled Dorothy joining O'Neill at a Village restaurant one night, bringing with her two seedy, tough, middle-aged men whom she had found on the icy steps of St. Joseph's Church and brought along to thaw out while having a drink at her expense. Dorothy ordered three rye whiskeys and proceeded to sing the tragic ballad of "Frankie and Johnny." She sometimes sang at The Golden Swan as well. Agnes recalled how fascinated O'Neill was at such moments, "moving slowly around, his dark eyes alive and pleased, admiring Dorothy's strange almost staccato singing." Agnes also found Dorothy impressive. "I saw at once that this girl was a personality, an unusual one." Dorothy's face, she said, was especially attractive in candlelight, which "brought out the long classic line of her jaw and the ends of her tousled hair."

O'Neill enjoyed reciting poetry, and the poem Dorothy best loved him to repeat was Francis Thompson's "The Hound of Heaven" which described God's tireless pursuit of each person's soul:

> I fled Him down the nights and down the days,
> I fled Him down the arches of the years;
> I fled Him down the labyrinthine ways
> Of my own mind . . .

O'Neill would recite the whole of the poem, sitting across from Dorothy, "looking dour and black," Dorothy remembered, "his head sunk on his chest," sighing out the words:

> And now my heart is as a broken fount,
> Wherein tear-drippings stagnate . . .

Her own loneliness for God often drew Dorothy into St. Joseph's Church on Sixth Avenue where she experienced a kind of at-homeness and consolation. While she knew very little about Catholic belief, she felt some comfort being in a place set aside for prayer. It was reassuring to be among people who came in for some quiet minutes, their heads bowed toward the consecrated bread hidden beyond the altar that in some mysterious way had been made one with Christ during the Mass.

O'Neill understood.

Dorothy absorbed him into her love of the city. Together they walked in the late hours, stopping at various taverns. Sometimes she put O'Neill to bed, drunk and shaking with the terrors that often wracked him, and (as she told a friend late in her life) held him in her arms until he fell asleep. He hoped for more than motherly comfort and one night asked her, "Dorothy, do you want to surrender your virginity?" It wasn't what she wanted. What she seems to have valued in O'Neill was being with someone whose loneliness resembled her own. He was the only one in her circle of friends who shared something of the need which drove her into churches. Others around her seemed sustained by anti-war or feminist convictions, by devotion to revolution, by art, by writing and reading, by social life and love affairs. For her such things were important, but not enough.

She had her own terrors to live with. Not yet twenty, she had left home and college, had moved from apartment to apartment in New York, walked out on her job at *The Call*, seen *The Masses* go under and with it another job, been in jail and now the biggest war in history was being fought in Europe. Everything seemed to be disintegrating.

One night early in 1918 a death occurred which drove home to her the need for a more positive engagement. A young man she knew only slightly discovered the woman he wanted to marry had fallen in love with someone else. Drunk and despairing at the end of what was supposed to have been a party, he took an overdose of heroin. "He died in my arms," Dorothy told Agnes Boulton and O'Neill shortly afterward, hardly able to speak through the grief she felt.

Kings County Hospital

"What good am I doing my fellow man," Dorothy wrote a friend. "They are sick and there are not enough nurses to care for them. . . . It's the poor that are suffering. I've got to care for them." In the spring of 1918, she began training as a nurse at Kings County Hospital in Brooklyn: changing bed pans, giving sponge baths and alcohol rubs, taking temperatures, administering injections and enemas, changing dressings, keeping charts, and dispensing medication. Making wrinkle-free beds was an especially hard-won craft, "more difficult," Dorothy decided, "than writing a book review." Her days of drinking late and sleeping late were abruptly over. The hospital's twelve-hour work day began promptly at six in the morning. Among a dozen probationers, Dorothy was one of six to survive the first month. Because an influenza epidemic was raging, the burden of work got progressively worse. By October, eight to ten shaking patients arrived each day, often collapsing as they reached the ward, some dying the same day.

It had been six years since Dorothy started wheeling her baby brother in slum neighborhoods instead of parks, feeling a first sense of vocation with those in need. Now they were central rather than incidental to her life. She was no longer just an observer or a reporter. Those who were suffering were in her care half of each day, and she began to know them by name.

There was Mary Windsor, age fifty, who was dying slowly, "looking out of wide grey eyes, looking at the death she saw so plainly, with a dull wonder."

Irma was a young woman facing death. "Her finely shaped mouth was always contorted with pain and there was a fierce protesting light in her eyes. The lines that agony had drawn in the ivory skin were like those of passion. She might have been clutching a lover in a last embrace, knowing that when he rose from the bed he would go out and close the door forever. There was the smell of death around her . . . and there was no one to bring her flowers to deaden it."

Granny, age 94, furious at being bathed, screamed and clawed at the nurses who approached her with soap and water. It was done only out of love, one nurse explained. "Love be damned," Granny replied in exulting defiance. Her greatest torture wasn't soap, Dorothy discovered, but the

33

hospital rule that had stripped Granny of her wig, leaving her in the ward with nothing but a cap which tended to slip over one ear, "displaying a large bald spot surrounded by a queer fringe of grey hair which was matted and awry, standing up like a field of ferns."

It was a patient such as Granny who once sent Dorothy running from the ward, her uniform filthy from the bedpan that had been hurled at her. One of the senior nurses found her crying in the washroom and with great gentleness talked with Dorothy about "the responsibilities of the nurse and the dignity of her profession and 'the sacrament of duty.' "

Still more difficult was a bearded woman with no breasts who spat at nurses who came too close. She was "filthy in her habits so that she constantly needed to be cleaned." Braving her fury and spit, Dorothy had to tend her daily, gritting her teeth and holding her breath. But relief came from patients like Lora McAlister, twenty-eight years old, with auburn hair and brown eyes, who had broken her hip in a car accident. Suddenly doctors haunted her ward and the floor men weren't so hurried in their cleaning work. The ward became beautiful with flowers brought by visitors. Despite her severe injuries, Lora "powdered and primped and sewed ribbons on her night dress and sang until the ward was aglow. ... The sixty- and seventy-year-old women became conscious of their sex and were more willing to have their faces washed." They gave Dorothy money "to buy them sweet-smelling talcums and relatives appeared with dainty night dresses for them."

She found another delightful patient when she was transferred to the men's ward: Philip, a handsome, elderly man who had the gift of picking flowers that grew unseen by others in the air around his bed. With unhurried discrimination, he sniffed the blossoms and his hands touched their invisible stems, assembling a daily bouquet, presenting it to Dorothy with a courteous, grave smile when she brought him his medicine. Once she noticed him pulling at what must have been goldenrod, given its resistance. "If you try to break it, instead of tearing at it," the man in the next bed advised, "maybe you'll get it off." That worked, and Dorothy was given an armful of goldenrod.

Abortion

One of the hospital orderlies was Lionel Moise, who worked in the men's ward to which Dorothy had been transferred. He assisted Dorothy in such tasks as undressing longshoremen who were in no mood to wear hospital garb. During the influenza epidemic, he carted numerous dead bodies down to the hospital morgue. At times it seemed to Dorothy that she and Moise were "the only healthy young things in the entire ward." Moise, then twenty-eight, recounted an adventurous life that could have been a story by Jack London. Most recently he had been a cameraman with a movie crew working in Latin America. He had worked as a deckhand on a freighter. At a saloon on the Brooklyn waterfront, he had been drugged, robbed and left unconscious on the streets. When he woke up, he was in a bed in Kings County Hospital, bruised and suffering pneumonia. He signed on as an orderly once he was out of bed in order to work off his hospital bill.

Moise was an utterly self-possessed man with a commanding manner. His face, which bore evidence of brawls he had taken part in, reminded Dorothy of the cherished postcard she had of a bust of Amenemhat III, the Egyptian pharaoh. Moise had no doubt that despite recent bad luck, he would make his way in the world. (Later on he became a successful journalist, working on such papers as *The Chicago Tribune* and *The San Francisco Examiner*. During a stretch with *The Kansas City Star*, in his home state, he was rewrite man for a staff that included Ernest Hemingway. Moise impressed Hemingway, who recalled that Moise "could carry four stories in his head and go to the telephone and take a fifth and then write all five at full speed to catch an edition. There was something alive in each one. He was always the highest paid man on every paper he worked on. ... He was tall and thick and had long arms and big hands.")

Dorothy, then twenty, found him captivating. For the first time in her life she fell deeply and incautiously in love. It was a "fatal attraction," she wrote soon after the event, and she didn't hesitate to tell him so. Moise assured her he wasn't the right type. "You should wait for some nice young man who will marry you and buy you a rubber tree and give you babies." For himself, he was opposed to marriage or anything resembling it; he didn't want either wives or children impeding his freedom. His objections in no

35

way arrested Dorothy's passion. She treasured the bits of time they had together in her long day and dared to imagine a future which they could share. When Moise left the hospital in September, Dorothy took leave and soon after moved into the apartment he had rented on 35th Street in Manhattan. Moise was earning $50 a week acting the part of a drunkard in a play that was about to open.

Moise accepted Dorothy, but on repressive terms. She wasn't to work, not even to write, but only to be "his woman." She made herself at home, made the apartment more attractive, repaired his clothes, darned his socks, and sewed clothing for herself, sometimes from silk remnants she bought cheaply. Cooking was the one domestic task Moise was willing to share.

When she renewed her Village friendships with Mike Gold, Peggy Baird and others, she discovered that Moise became explosively jealous. They first separated when he noticed her hand resting on the shoulder of the man sitting next to her in a cafe. He stormed out, saying, "I'll leave you here to embrace the gentleman on your right."

Dorothy was devastated by the abrupt severance. She found refuge in the following days with various friends. It was while staying in a room in Greenwich Village that she was dragged unconscious after another resident smelled gas coming from under her door. Whether it was by despair or accident is unclear, but the hose to a gas heater had been disconnected.

Early in 1919, the affair resumed, Dorothy more desperate than ever to hold Moise. She wished that her "death would coincide" with the moment Moise stopped loving her.

Though Dorothy had been associated with publications promoting birth control, in her affair with Moise she made no effort to prevent the conception of a child, despite his warning that he would leave if she had a child. In the summer Dorothy discovered she was pregnant and contemplated various possibilities. She couldn't bear to sign into a home for unwed mothers—it was too humiliating. Given the tension between John Day and herself, she couldn't return home. She couldn't tell Moise or he would leave. Abortion, though illegal, seemed the only course. She obtained the name of an abortionist but couldn't bring herself to make an appointment.

In an autobiographical novel written in 1921, she described herself peering at infants in baby carriages and watching children in the parks. From her apartment window, she studied two sisters playing in the yard—a five-year-old who held up her skirts and sang the Missouri Waltz and a two-year-old who occasionally turned her round face to the sky and fell "into a perfect trance of happiness."

She tried to convince herself that it was only Moise she wanted, not a child, and that "perfect love precluded the idea of children." Lovers only need each other. And if they were no longer lovers, if he left her, how could she afford a child? How would the two of them live? And wasn't it selfish to bring children into the world unless they're going to have a fair chance at happiness? Doesn't a child deserve and need a father?

Moise heard none of these questions. Dorothy told him she was pregnant only in the early fall, the day he told her he had been offered a job in Caracas and was leaving in a week. She blurted out her desperate news. He felt sorry, but would still be leaving. He advised her to have an abortion. Dorothy couldn't argue. She wept.

According to Dorothy's novel, the operation occurred in an apartment on the Upper East Side. A surgical instrument cut the child from the lining of her womb. For several hours there were painful contractions, one spasm every three minutes. Finally, a half-year-old child was born dead.

If Dorothy's novel is as biographically accurate in the account of the abortion as it is on many other subjects, Moise had promised to meet her afterward, but he never showed up. At the apartment on 35th Street that night, she found a letter in which he reminded her that millions of women had had the same experience. He left some money and hoped she would get "comfortably married to a rich man." This is exactly what she did.

Breaking Free

A few months after the abortion, in the early spring of 1920, Dorothy married Berkeley Tobey, a founder of the Literary Guild, and one of the wealthier inhabitants of Greenwich Village, living in a large apartment overlooking Washington Square Park. He was twenty years her senior. It was, Dorothy wrote, a "marriage on the rebound."

That summer Tobey took Dorothy to Europe. In London she "walked and took bus rides and explored and thought of DeQuincey and Dickens." In Paris her imagination put her in the company of Victor Hugo, Balzac and Maupassant. But it was Italy that most delighted her and offered her more than literary associations. "The six months I spent in Capri meant that forever after, the smell of Italian cooking, the sound of buzzing flies, the loud voices of my Italian neighbors, the taste of spaghetti and polenta and the sour red wine brought me back to the months I spent beside the Mediterranean."

During her year in Europe, Dorothy wrote *The Eleventh Virgin*, an autobiography with a thin fictional veneer. Her mother's name was left unchanged. Her sister Della became Adele. Rayna was changed to Regina. Mike Gold was dubbed Ivan, no doubt because of his enthusiasm for Russia. *The Call* became *The Clarion* and *The Masses* was renamed *The Flame*. The last chapters were the story of her affair with Moise, culminating in the abortion and his departure.

Even married and in Europe, Dorothy was by no means through with Moise. "I'm still in love," she confides in the book's epilogue.

The marriage with Tobey was over by the following summer, when Dorothy returned to America and went directly to Chicago, where Moise had a job on a city newspaper. Dorothy rented a room with a student and took whatever work she could find: clerk at Montgomery Ward's, copyholder to a proofreader, auxiliary at the Public Library, cashier at a restaurant, and model for life drawing classes. Finally she returned to employment with a radical journal as secretary to Robert Minor, editor of the newly founded monthly, *The Liberator*, a Communist publication. Many of the editors, writers and artists who had been associated with *The Masses* were now involved with *The Liberator*, and undoubtedly its anti-war position and its open advocacy of revolution occasioned close government surveillance. "At this moment of writing," Robert Minor said repeatedly in letters that he dictated to Dorothy, "there is a man standing in the doorway across the street who has been shadowing me for the past week."

Among other locations being watched closely was a building in the Skid Row section of Chicago's West Side where the Wobblies had offices and a printing press. Upstairs there were hospitality rooms for visitors and local people in need. From time to time Dorothy stayed there, including one night in late July 1922 when she brought with her Mae Cramer. "We were both in love with the same man," Dorothy later wrote. Just the day before Mae had tried to kill herself with an overdose of drugs because things were going badly between herself and Moise.

It happened that night that the police "Red Squad" raided the house in one of the radical roundups authorized by U.S. Attorney General A. Mitchell Palmer and his special assistant, J. Edgar Hoover. "We were undressed and getting into bed," Dorothy recalled, "when a knock came at the door and four men burst in telling us we were under arrest for being inmates of a disorderly house." A disorderly house was the legal term for a place of prostitution and other illegal activities. For Dorothy it was an utterly terrifying experience. When she had been arrested in Washington, the event had been carried out as if it were a ballet. Arrest and imprisonment had been chosen to make Americans think about the exclusion of women from the democratic process. Now she was seized suddenly in the night, made to dress in front of armed men, and herded roughly into a police van.

While the charges were dropped after two days, this second experience of prison, for all its brevity, impressed her more than the first with the ugliness and brutality of prison. "We were stripped naked. We were given prison clothes and put in cells. . . . In the next cell to me there was a drug addict who beat her head against the bars and howled like a wild animal. I have never heard such anguish, such unspeakable suffering. No woman in childbirth, no cancer patient, no one in that long year I had spent in Kings County Hospital had revealed such suffering as this." Yet she came to regard the experience with thanks. "I am glad indeed that I had it," she wrote, because of the taste it gave her of what happened "to thousands who had worked for labor—hotel workers, miners, the textile workers—throughout the country." Workers had withheld their labor, joined picket lines at factory gates, been beaten and sometimes were maimed and killed. By the thousands they were thrown into jails, and were treated by the press with contempt. "Every strike was an unjust strike according to the newspapers, and every strike ended in failure according to the same papers. The reader never took into account the slow and steady gains, wrung reluctantly from the employer by virtue of every one of these strikes."

After her release, Dorothy was hired as a reporter for the City News Bureau, covering the Children's Court, the Court of Domestic Relations, and the Morals Court. At the same time she rented a room in a Catholic household, living with three women her own age for whom Mass was a part of every Sunday and special holy day, and for whom prayer was part of daily life. Two of the women were also in love, but weren't sleeping with the men they hoped to marry though it was evident to Dorothy how much they wanted to. In seeing their daily life and the role of faith in it, she began to feel "that Catholicism was something rich and real and fascinating. . . . I saw them wrestling with moral problems, with the principles by which they lived, and this made them noble jn my eyes." Seeing them at prayer, at the table and by their beds, she realized that "worship, adoration, thanksgiving, supplication—these were the noblest acts of which we are capable in this life." Not for the first time, she felt drawn to the Catholic Church, the Church of immigrants and the masses of poor brought together in Christ.

It was in the midst of this slow inner opening, the winter of 1922–1923, that Dorothy finally broke free of her attraction to Moise. When her friend Mary Gordon decided to move south to New Orleans, Dorothy joined her. At the same time, she received news from Albert and Charles Boni, the publishers in Greenwich Village to whom she had submitted her manuscript, that *The Eleventh Virgin* had been accepted.

The Beach House

Dorothy and Mary found an apartment on St. Peter's Street in New Orleans' French Quarter, a district splendid in its raiment of wrought-iron balconies. Dorothy got a job reporting for *The New Orleans Item*, for which she did a series on "taxi dancers"—dancers for hire in local night spots. She joined the ranks of the taxi dancers herself and one night was assaulted by some of them, ending up with a black eye. One story was headlined, "Dance Halls Flooded by Dope, Drink."

Just down the street from her apartment was Saint Louis Cathedral, where Dorothy went to pray and often attended the evening Benediction service. She was pleased when her roommate, a Communist, expressed her sympathy by giving Dorothy a rosary.

Her book was published in the spring, but received poor press notices. *The New York Times'* reviewer recognized that it was more a work of autobiography than fiction and dismissed it as an example of the "truth at any cost" school of writing. "Truth is so prominent that there is practically nothing else." (Dorothy herself came to regard *The Eleventh Virgin* as "a very bad book" and bitterly regretted its publication.) The book found few readers and there was no second printing. The royalties were slight. Yet the book did make a great deal of money both for Dorothy and the publisher when a movie company in Hollywood bought the film rights for $5,000, though no film was ever produced. Dorothy's share was only half, but even that was a small fortune. Up to that time she and her roommate had been happy to have quarters for the coin-operated gas meter in their apartment kitchen. "The gas was apt to run out," Dorothy recalled, "just when we had spent our last cent on a rabbit stew which took hours to boil."

In April 1924, a published author with money from Hollywood in hand, Dorothy returned to New York where she found a warm welcome and hospitality from Peggy Baird. Peggy had married essayist Malcolm Cowley, and their apartment on Bank Street in Greenwich Village was a gathering place for writers and radicals. The poet Hart Crane was a frequent visitor. Caroline Gordon and Allen Tate lived across the street. The makings for elaborate discussion and debate were constantly at hand. A particular conversation involving Malcolm Cowley, the music critic Kenneth Burke and novelist John Dos Passos lingered in Dorothy's memory "because I could not understand a word of it."

Peggy realized that Dorothy's money was gradually evaporating and suggested that it would be better spent buying a quiet place to write. Early in 1924 the two took the ferry to Staten Island and before the day had ended Dorothy had found and bought a fisherman's cottage fronting the beach.

It was about the same time, and again through Peggy and her husband, that Dorothy met Forster Batterham, "an anarchist, an Englishman by descent, and a biologist," in Dorothy's words. Forster was tall, lean, with a high forehead under sandy hair, a lover of the outdoors, a gifted fisherman, and a visceral opponent of all big institutions. He approved of neither marriage nor religion.

Dorothy fell in love with him. It was quite mutual and, in very little time, they agreed to live together part-time. She moved into her beach house, wrote serial fiction for a newspaper syndicate, and Forster joined her on weekends. For most of the week, the house was a writer's hermitage. Dorothy had begun four of the most joyful years of her life.

She loved the sounds—the living sounds of the sea, the wind, of children playing on the beach, the singing of birds, the cries of gulls. The air, too, was a marvel—not reeking of trucks, buses and tenements, but scrubbed clean, seeming fresh from heaven. Every day there were walks along the beach collecting driftwood delivered by the tides. "The little house was furnished very simply with a driftwood stove in one corner, plenty of books, comfortable chairs and couches. My writing table faced the window where I could look out at the water all day. On the walls hung the fruits of our collecting: horseshoe crabs, spider crabs, the shell of a huge sea turtle, whelks' cocoons, hanging like false curls, several mounted fish heads, boards covered with starfish, sea horses, pipe and file fish, all picked up in little pools at low tide."

There were good neighbors, including Italians, Belgians, and a family of Russian and Romanian Jews. Among them were bootleggers and fishermen. For all their differences of temperament and way of life, they got on with each other. Events and misunderstandings that might have ignited undying enmity were excused on the grounds of nationality.

In one tiny shack lived a beachcomber named Lefty, who slept with his crab traps and clam forks and tried to live without money, as he only spent it drinking. "Money is bad for me, I know it," he told Dorothy. "I can trade my fish and clams for fuel and food and what else do I need?" He kept a special steamer chair for Dorothy's use and shared his meals gladly: coffee, buttered toast with fried mushrooms, steamed clams, and clam juice, which he said was the best thing for a hangover. Lefty, like so many in the neighborhood, was poor, often penniless, and yet he wasn't humiliated or brutalized by poverty.

Dorothy was reading a book of essays by William James as she sat on the beach one day and was impressed with his proposal that the only way to undo the damage done by the ideal of wealth-getting was to revive belief in poverty as a worthy religious vocation: "The praises of poverty need once more to be boldly sung," James wrote. "We have grown literally afraid to be poor. We despise anyone who elects to be poor in order to simplify and save his inner life. If he does not join the general scramble, we deem him spiritless and lacking in ambition. We have lost the power even of imagining what the ancient realization of poverty could have meant; the liberation from material attachments, the unbribed soul."

Proof of the text was given by Lefty, Dorothy realized, and by Forster as well, "who refused to do other than live from day to day and insisted on his freedom of body and soul." He worked, but just enough to pay for his share in their household expenses, and never spent money if he could help it.

With an English love for the outdoors, she wrote, "he used to insist on walks no matter how cold or rainy the day, and this dragging me away from my books, from my lethargy, into the open, into the country, made me begin to breathe. If breath is life, then I was beginning to be full of it because of him."

Listening to Forster read aloud from *The New York Times* over the breakfast table, Dorothy recovered her awareness of the world beyond the beach, her books, the cottage and her neighbors. "Usually if anyone reads aloud to you, you can listen or not, at will, but the vehemence and passion of Forster's interest and his rebellion at all injustice forced me to realize the situation with him." For Forster, however, his obsession with news only seemed to confirm him in his bitterness with "the blundering of his fellow creatures. He loved nature with a sensuous passion and he loved birds and beasts and children because they were not men."

Certainly he loved Dorothy. It warmed her to remember how he would come in smelling of salt air from a cold night, having dug bait at low tide in the moonlight, and "hold me close to him in silence." And the love was shared fully. "I loved him in every way, as a wife, as a mother even. I loved him for all he knew and pitied him for all he didn't know. I loved him for the odds and ends I had to fish out of his sweater pockets and for the sand and shells he brought in with his fishing. I loved his lean and cold body as he got into bed smelling of the sea, and I loved his integrity and stubborn pride."

It pained her that he was so set against "the institution of family and the tyranny of love" and that he would never let her forget "that this was a comradeship rather than a marriage." At times it seemed senseless that they were together at all, "since he lived with me as though he were living alone."

Her own belief in the existence of God had become definite. She pitied Forster for not knowing God's presence within all that he loved so wholly and desperately, the creation whose beauty is a confession of God. He could not understand, share or welcome her pleasure in hearing the bells of the nearby chapel of St. Joseph's as it tolled the Angelus morning and night. "Forster, the inarticulate, became garrulous only in wrath . . . caused by my absorption in the supernatural rather than the natural, the unseen rather than the seen." They quarreled, but not bitterly. Dorothy well understood Forster's angry rejection of churches and all that they claimed to represent, define, and judge. She knew arguments were powerless. In any event, her own vague religious impulses were still more troubling than comforting in her own life. She belonged to no church. She was ill at ease with religious doctrines. But she was deeply aware of God's presence and couldn't ban that awareness from her thoughts or silence it in her speech. "How can there be no God," she told Forster, "when there are all these beautiful things?"

Pregnancy and Faith

Dorothy still had the rosary she had been given years before in New Orleans. In the spring of 1925, during daily walks to the post office in the nearby village of Huguenot, she began using it as a means of prayer. "Maybe I did not say it correctly, but I kept on saying it because it made me happy." While walking the beach at low tide in search of driftwood for the stove, she often silently recited the words of the *Te Deum*, the ancient hymn to the Trinity Dorothy had learned in the Episcopal church that she had attended as a child in Chicago:

> We praise thee, O God; we acknowledge thee to be the Lord.
> All the earth doth worship thee, the Father everlasting. . . .
> Heaven and earth are full of the Majesty of thy glory. . . .
> Thou art the King of Glory, O Christ.
> Thou art the everlasting Son of the Father.
> When thou tookest thee to deliver man, thou didst hum-
>   ble thyself to be born of a Virgin.
> When thou hadst overcome the sharpness of death, thou didst
>   open the Kingdom of heaven to all believers. . . .
> O Lord, in thee have I trusted; let me never be confounded.

The regal Shakespearean English seemed like stone smoothed and shaped by an ancient stream. Each sentence was beautiful to say, a joy to the tongue.

Doing housework within her cottage, her attention often drifted toward a small statue of Mary. "I found myself addressing the Blessed Virgin and turning toward her statue."

She knew that some of her friends would find her hidden, inner life a delusion. For them it was obvious and not just a tenet of Marxism that prayer and religion were "the opiate of the people." Prayer was the numbing of conscience rather than its sharpening, an evasion of reality, an engagement in the mentality of passivity and bondage to which so many were driven by exhaustion, injustice and sorrow. Yet the driving force of prayer in her own life, Dorothy realized, was gratitude and joy. "I am praying because I am happy, not because I am unhappy. I did not turn to

God in unhappiness, in grief, in despair—to get consolation, to get something. . . ."

When she tried to pray on her knees, arguments against prayer overwhelmed her thoughts. But whenever she set out walking—no matter what the direction, the purpose, the hour, the distance or the weather—the debate was stilled and she found it impossible *not* to pray. Words of praise seemed to recite themselves with each step and only ceased when she was so filled with exultation that she was beyond words and even thought. "There had been other periods of intense joy but seldom had there been the quiet beauty and happiness I felt now. I had thought all those years that I had freedom, but now I felt that I had never known real freedom nor even had the knowledge of what freedom meant."

Despite Forster's bewilderment and irritation, she began going to Mass on Sunday mornings. Even when audible, the Latin was incomprehensible, the ritual baffling, and yet she found a special peace just in being present.

The great absence in her life was motherhood. "For a long time I had thought I could not bear a child, and the longing in my heart for a baby had been growing. My home, I felt, was not a home without one. The simple joys of the kitchen and garden brought sadness with them because I felt myself unfruitful, barren. No matter how much one was loved or one loved, that love was lonely without a child. It was incomplete."

In the five years since the abortion, there had been no second conception. Dorothy had concluded she was one of those for whom abortion had damaged the womb in such a way that pregnancy was impossible.

Then in June she found she was carrying a child. "I will never forget my blissful joy when I was first sure." The day of certainty happened to coincide with a trip to Tottenville to see a circus. "We brought dandelion wine and pickled eels and good homemade bread and butter. . . . I remember . . . feeling so much in love, so settled, so secure that I now had found what I was looking for."

Forster's response was quite different. He didn't believe "in bringing children into such a world." The awful responsibility of parenthood frightened him. And a child would be, like God and prayer, still another barrier between himself and Dorothy.

But nothing could banish Dorothy's sense that what was happening within her was marvelous, a miracle twice over. "I found myself, a barren woman, the joyful mother of children."

She gave up worrying about her attraction to prayer and searched out books on the religious life, among them *The Imitation of Christ*, by Thomas à Kempis, and William James' *The Varieties of Religious Experience*, and a life of Teresa of Avila, the sixteenth-century Spanish mystic and reformer, a saint with whom Dorothy readily identified. "Teresa liked to read novels when she was a young girl," Dorothy wrote, "and she wore a bright red dress when she entered the convent. Later she became the founder of many religious communities. When sisters in her care became melancholy, St.

Teresa responded by ordering steaks for the community meal, and on occasion took up castanets and danced." Though Teresa complained that "life is like a night spent at an uncomfortable inn," she sought to make the inn contain reminders of heaven. She had a passionate faith, so durable and good humored that she could both argue with and tease her Creator. When thrown from a donkey while crossing a stream, she heard Christ say to her, "That is how I treat my friends." She responded, "No wonder you have so few!"

On March 4, 1926, Tamar Theresa was born. Very quickly Dorothy wrote about her labor and delivery in an essay, "Having a Baby," for *New Masses*, the Communist monthly. "I wanted to share my joy with the world," she wrote in her autobiography, "and was glad to write that joy for a workers' magazine because it was a joy all women knew, no matter what their grief at poverty, unemployment and class war. The article so appealed to my Marxist friends that the account was printed all over the world in workers' papers. Diego Rivera, when I met him some four years afterward in Mexico, greeted me as the author of it. And Mike Gold, who was at that time editor of *New Masses*, said it had been printed in many Soviet newspapers and that I had rubles awaiting me in Moscow."

It was Tamar that occasioned Dorothy's conversion. "No human creature could receive or contain so vast a flood of love and joy as I often felt after the birth of my child. With this came the need to worship, to adore."

She knew association with any church, and especially the Catholic Church, would be objectionable to Forster and to nearly every friend she had. They regarded the Church as an institution that blessed injustice, that still practiced repression, and that had never repented its periods of torturing those suspected of heresy and burning those who were condemned. But Dorothy's attraction was based on her own experience and need, not on history or argument.

"I had heard many say that they wanted to worship God in their own way and did not need a Church in which to praise Him, nor a body of people with whom to associate themselves. But I did not agree to this. My whole experience as a radical, my whole makeup, led me to want to associate with others, with the masses, in loving and praising God. Without even looking into the claims of the Catholic Church, I was willing to admit that for me she was the one true Church. She had come down through the centuries since the time of Peter, and far from being dead, she claimed and held the allegiance of the masses of people in all the cities where I had lived. They poured in and out of her doors on Sundays and holy days."

Coming into the Church seemed the real fruit of those many long walks of joyous prayer. "What a driving power joy is! When I was unhappy and repentant in the past I turned to God, but it was my joy at having given birth to a child that made me do something definite." The Church and faith were interwoven, and she could think of nothing more precious to found her daughter's life upon than these. "I did not want my child to flounder as I had often floundered," Dorothy commented in some notes written in later years. "I wanted to believe, and I wanted my child to believe, and if belonging to a Church would give her so inestimable a grace as faith in God, and the companionable love of the Saints, then the thing to do was to have her baptized a Catholic. She would be incorporated into the Church; it was to be hoped she would grow in wisdom and grace and in following the footsteps of Jesus and have all the safeguards and helps that a universal Church would give."

When Dorothy saw an elderly nun walking near St. Joseph's Home, an institution for orphans and unwed mothers, she didn't hesitate to approach her. "I went up to her breathlessly and asked her how I could have my child baptized. She was not at all reticent about asking questions and not at all surprised at my desires." Sister Aloysia began to visit the beach house three times each week, drilling Dorothy in memorized questions and answers about the rudiments of Catholic teaching, and challenging Dorothy to prepare herself as well as her daughter for life in the Catholic Church.

Baptism

Tamar was baptized in July 1927. Forster considered the ceremony all mumbo-jumbo and wouldn't be present, and his resistance to the religious direction in Dorothy's life became sharper. If he happened to be at home when Sister Aloysia dropped in, he slammed the door as he escaped with his fishing pole. Arguments and brief separations became common events, though Forster always returned to Dorothy in boyish repentance.

Dorothy dreaded the prospect of life alone and nursed a desperate hope that Forster might eventually develop some understanding and sympathy for her religious faith, and that in time he would become supportive enough so that they could formally marry. Her first marriage to Berkeley Tobey had not been a sacramental union and had no standing in the view of the Church. But the prospect of marriage in the Catholic Church was intolerable to Forster. He felt he would be both a liar and a hypocrite were he to take part in "any ceremony before officials of either Church or state."

In the meantime, while the two continued to live together without the sanction of marriage, her own reception into the Church had to be delayed.

Despite growing tensions between them, Tamar was a point of shared delight. Forster's earlier reservations about bringing children into the world had been swept away by the reality of his fascinating daughter.

By the fall, Tamar was old enough to insist on her place in adult activities. "She gets her little hands entangled in my knitting," Dorothy noted in her journal, "or mixed up in my typewriter keys." At the time Dorothy was writing a series of articles based on interviews with workers and the unemployed. Tamar loudly protested Dorothy's long hours spent writing and reading. "She feels that I am escaping from my duty when I become absorbed in them, and she feels she must recall me to it."

Dorothy became troubled with her self-imposed exile from the slums and wondered if she weren't too contented, "nestled into this scrap of land and filled with a hideous sense of possession." Both she and Forster suffered a shared anguish in August in the days leading up to the execution of Nicola Sacco and Bartolomeo Vanzetti, Italian immigrants and anarchists who had been condemned for robbery and murder in Massachusetts. Despite weighty evidence of their innocence, massive demonstrations, and appeals from many countries, the governor refused to commute the death sentence to life imprisonment. (A Massachusetts governor fifty years later issued a proclamation declaring Sacco and Vanzetti had been improperly tried.)

For both Dorothy and Forster, it was a ritual execution of people whose real crimes were their foreign origins, their radical beliefs, their commitment to the poor, and their indictment of the wealthy. For Dorothy, it was an event reminiscent of the crucifixion. She wept in reading Vanzetti's last letter from prison.

> [Sacco] and I never brought a morsel of bread to our mouths, from our childhood to today, which was not gained by the sweat of our brows. Never ...

> [We are called thieves, assassins and doomed, yet] if it had not been for these things I might have lived out my life talking on street corners to scorning men. I might have died, unmarked, unknown, a failure.

> This is our career and our triumph.

> Never in our full life could we hope to do such work for tolerance, for justice, for man's understanding of man, as we now do by accident.

> Our words, our lives, our pain — nothing.

> The taking of our lives — lives of a good shoe maker and a poor fish peddler — all!

> The last moment belongs to us — the agony is our triumph.

When the news of the executions was published, Dorothy remembered, the headlines were as large as those which announced the outbreak of the world war. "All the nation mourned. All the nation, I mean, that is made up of the poor, the worker, the trade unionist — those who felt most keenly the sense of solidarity — that very sense of solidarity which made me gradually understand the doctrine of the Mystical Body of Christ whereby we are members of one another."

Forster was so stricken that for days he lived as if dead himself, unable to eat or speak, utterly sickened by the cruelty of life and the heartlessness of those in power. No doubt it struck him that among the many institutions that stood by unprotesting while two poor men were electrocuted was the very Church to which Dorothy had attached herself.

One afternoon just after Christmas, their differences exploded once again, and again Forster stormed out the door. "When he returned, as he always had, I would not let him in the house; my heart was breaking with my own determination to make an end, once and for all, to the torture that we were enduring."

The same afternoon, she called the parish priest and made an appointment for her reception into the Catholic Church.

On December 28, after leaving Tamar with her sister Della, Dorothy went to the church in Tottenville. She had been baptized during childhood in the Episcopal Church, but was baptized again conditionally, and afterward went to confession. No friends were present except her godparent, Sister Aloysia.

But the long-awaited event gave her no consolation, as she contemplated the final break with Forster and its consequences for herself and Tamar. "I had no sense of peace, no joy, no conviction that what I was doing was right. It was just something that I had to do, a task to be gotten through."

Participating at her first Mass as a Catholic the next day, she felt wooden, like someone going through the motions. "I felt like a hypocrite as I got down on my knees, and shuddered at the thought of anyone seeing me." Was she not betraying the oppressed and the radical movement? "Here I was, going over to the opposition, because the Church was lined up with property, with the wealthy, with capitalism, with all the forces of reaction."

It pained her to see "businesslike priests" who seemed "more like Cain than Abel," who ignored the poor and never said a word about social injustice. Yet she was grateful that even they offered her access to the sacraments. She took comfort in knowing that there were other priests who lived poorly and "who gave their lives daily for their fellows." However often Christ seemed hidden rather than revealed by the Church, still it was Christ's Church. If the bishops and the clergy seemed often unaware of the poor, the poor were *in* the Church.

If only it was less a Church of charities and more a Church of social justice. "I felt that charity was a word to choke over. Who wanted charity? And it was not just human pride but a strong sense of man's dignity and worth, and what was due to him in justice, that made me resent rather than feel proud of so mighty a sum of Catholic institutions." It seemed all too often that the charities were hardly better than government agencies, heavy with bureaucracy and lacking a human touch.

"How I longed to make a synthesis reconciling body and soul, this world and the next."

Prayer in Washington

The five years following Dorothy's entrance into the Catholic Church centered on her search to find something that didn't exist: a way of supporting herself and Tamar through work which joined her religious faith, her commitment to social justice, and writing. Alternately, she thought of making a good deal of money. For part of 1928, she handled publicity for the Anti-Imperialist League, which was then campaigning for the end of U. S. military intervention in Central America and raising aid and medical supplies for the nationalist leader, General Augusto Sandino. It was a Communist-affiliated group with offices on Union Square. "I was so new a Catholic," Dorothy wrote in *Therese* more than thirty years later, "that I was still working for the committee some months after my baptism. 'I am in agreement with it,' I told my confessor, Father Zachary. 'We should not be sending our Marines to Nicaragua. I am in agreement with many of the social aims of Communism: From each according to his ability, to each according to his need.' Father Zachary could only quote Lenin to me, saying, 'Atheism is basic to Marxism.' He was the gentlest of confessors with me, who, at that time, was a female counterpart of Graham Greene's Quiet American, wanting to do good by violence."

During the same period, she began doing part-time work from her apartment for the MGM film company, writing summaries of new novels at six dollars per book.

Yet clearly there was some tension in Dorothy about achieving peaceful goals with violent means. In 1929, she found part-time work at the national office of the Fellowship of Reconciliation, the religious pacifist organization which was developing nonviolent methods of struggle in the labor and civil rights movements, and whose members committed themselves to refuse any part in warfare. At the time, the FOR was also working for the end of Washington's "gunboat diplomacy" in Latin America. Dorothy became a member, and remained in the FOR for the rest of her life, but she felt isolated as the only Catholic in an office otherwise staffed entirely by Protestants.

That summer, she and Tamar were able to return to Staten Island, where Dorothy had found a job near the beach house working as a cook for Catholic seminarians.

Her synopsis-writing for MGM continued, and an offer came to work in Hollywood writing film dialogue for the Pathé Motion Picture Company. She was offered what seemed a royal salary: $125 per week. Late in the summer of 1929, a few weeks before the crash of the stock market and the beginning of the Great Depression, Dorothy and Tamar boarded the train to California.

"Like all Hollywood authors, I thought of the money I would make that would free me to live the simple life in the future and work on a novel I was always writing."

At the Pathé studio, Dorothy had a private office, met with other screen writers, and attended private screen showings. But she felt very isolated. It was a lonely and empty time that lasted only three months.

Early in 1930, Dorothy left California for Mexico City in a newly acquired Ford Model T and rented a room from a one-armed woman whose daughter sold stockings from a pushcart in a nearby park. For the first time, Dorothy was living amidst people for whom Catholicism was integral to life. Her fascination with the Mexican people and their faith found expression in a series of articles she wrote for *Commonweal*, a Catholic weekly edited by laypeople in New York. The drama and theater in liturgy astonished her: processions with life-size statues, churches overflowing with people, and the deep penetration of vivid symbols of belief from the church to the home. In one Easter Mass, tens of thousands of flower petals showered continuously on the brightly dressed Indians packed into the church she attended. She also encountered hostility to religion, especially among radical intellectuals such as the artist Diego Rivera. Dorothy sympathized with some of their criticisms, only wishing they could glimpse the Church through the eyes of the faithful, so many of whom were the poor.

After half a year, when Tamar contracted malaria, Dorothy decided to return to New York.

The Great Depression was in its second year. "More and more people were losing their jobs, more families were being evicted, the Unemployed Councils were being formed by the Communist groups and the Workers Alliance sprang into existence. It was time for pressure groups, for direct action, and radicalism was thriving among all groups except Catholics. I felt out of it. There was Catholic membership in all these groups, of course, but no Catholic leadership. It was that very year that Pope Pius XI said sadly, 'The workers of the world are lost to the Church.' "

Dorothy herself felt no capacity for leadership nor had she a clear idea of where a leader ought to be heading. She saw herself only as a bystander, a diarist, a reporter, a literate witness. The longing that had drawn her toward the Catholic Church was undiminished, but was subject to growing anguish with her own passivity. At the advice of a priest who heard her weekly confession, she gave up her custom of sleeping as late as her work and parenthood allowed and began her lifelong practice of daily Mass and Communion. On Saturday nights, she took part in Benediction, a special service of thanksgiving for the presence of Christ in bread consecrated at Mass. She returned to the writings of St. Teresa of Avila.

In the colder months, she lived in Manhattan, renting space in an Italian and German neighborhood on the Lower East Side. With warmer weather, she returned to the beach house on Staten Island. In her absence friends had used it, letting the garden fall to weeds and substituting fish hooks for the crucifix on the wall.

Whether in Manhattan or Staten Island, her writing continued: another autobiographical novel was completed but found no publisher; she wrote a gardening column for Staten Island's daily newspaper, *The Advance*; there were occasional articles for Catholic magazines, especially *Commonweal* and *America*, the latter a weekly edited by Jesuits at Fordham University.

It was for *Commonweal* and *America* that Dorothy reported the Hunger March, an event that proved a turning point in her life.

Union Square, hub of so many radical events, was the point of departure November 30, 1932 for about six hundred jobless marchers destined for Washington. The popular press treated the event as a rag-tag parade of dangerous radicals whose demonstration was evidence of Red revolution. Little attention was given the marchers' proposals: jobs, unemployment insurance, old-age pensions, relief for mothers and children, health care and housing for those who had lost everything. Hostility along the way reached a crescendo in Wilmington, Delaware, where police hurled tear gas canisters through the windows of a Protestant church which had had the courage to open its doors to the marchers. Those escaping the gas were clubbed down and the suspected leaders were thrown into police vans and taken to jail. Despite delays, the Hunger March was able to press on.

When the swelling assembly reached the edge of Washington, barricades were put across the highway. The demonstration was forbidden to enter the capital. Refusing to disband, the marchers camped out for three days and nights despite bitter weather and encirclement by armed police. Route 1 was closed to traffic. Each day headlines warned of a Communist menace which bore little resemblance to the actual people who had endured insults and violence to dramatize the hardships and needs of the unemployed. Dorothy was appalled by the role of the press. "If there was not a story, the newspapers would make a story. ... The newspaper reporters were infected by their own journalism and began to beg editors to give them tear-gas masks before they went out to interview the leaders of the unemployed marchers."

Yet in the end, on December 8, the police moved the barricades and stood aside. "On a bright sunny day the ragged horde triumphantly with banners flying, with lettered slogans mounted on sticks, paraded three-thousand-strong through the tree-flanked streets of Washington. I stood on the curb and watched them, joy and pride in the courage of this band of men and women mounting in my heart."

She felt bitterness as well. She knew the Hunger March had been organ-

Dorothy and her sister Della in Chicago.

" 'All my life I have been haunted by God,' a character in one of Dostoyevsky's books says. And that is the way it was with me."

Dorothy's mother,
Grace Satterlee Day.

"In the family, the name of God was never mentioned."

John Day, Sr., with Dorothy's older brother, Donald.

"I wanted a Lord who would scourge the moneylenders out of the temple, and I wanted to help all those who raised their hand against oppression."

Young Dorothy Day at the time of her arrival in New York.

In 1917, on the staff of *The Call*, a socialist newspaper that opposed U.S. entry in World War I.

"The man I loved, with whom I entered into a common-law marriage, was an anarchist, an Englishman by descent, and a biologist."

Dorothy with Forster Batterham on the beach on Staten Island.

Courtesy Tamar Hennessy

Courtesy Tamar Hennessy

"No human creature could receive or contain so vast a flood of love and joy as I often felt after the birth of my child. With this came the need to worship, to adore."

Dorothy with Tamar Teresa in 1926.

*"I had become con-
vinced that I would
become a Catholic,
and yet I felt I was
betraying the class
to which I belonged,
the workers, the
poor of the world
with whom Christ
spent His life."*

Courtesy Tamar Hennessy

Dorothy and Tamar on the beach, 1927.

Courtesy Tamar Hennessy

*"Becoming a Catholic would
mean facing life alone, and I
clung to family life."*

Dorothy with her sister
Della in 1928. Tamar is in
the center.

Dorothy and Tamar,
c. 1932.

Marquette University Archives

"How I longed to make a synthesis reconciling body and soul, this world and the next . . ."

Dorothy with her sister-in-law Tessa De Aragon, 1932.

Courtesy Tamar Hennessy

"When I walked into my apartment, I found waiting for me a short, stocky man in his mid-fifties, as ragged and rugged as any of the marchers I had left . . . This man introduced himself briefly: 'I am Peter Maurin.' "

Maurin in front of St. Joseph's House on Mott St. in the early 1930s.

Marquette University Archives

"We would sell the paper for a cent a copy, to make it so cheap that anyone could afford to buy it."

Early copies of *The Catholic Worker* are distributed in Union Square.

Marquette University Archives

"We are working for 'a new heaven and a new earth, wherein justice dwelleth' We are trying to say with action, 'Thy will be done on earth as it is in heaven' We are working for a Christian social order."

Dorothy and Catholic Worker staff in front of the newspaper headquarters.

"What right has any one of us to security when God's poor are suffering? What right have I to sleep in a comfortable bed when so many are sleeping in the shadows of buildings here in this neighborhood?"

Breadline in front of the Catholic Worker, c. 1938.

"What we would like to do is change the world—make it a little simpler for people to feed, clothe, and shelter themselves as God intended them to do."

Tamar (standing at left), Dorothy, and Peter Maurin, c. 1935.

Marquette University Archives

Maryknoll Archives

"Love and ever more love is the only solution to every problem that comes up."

Dorothy in the early years of the CW.

"There was a quiet and perfect peace and a happiness so deep and strong and thankful that even my words of prayer seemed inadequate to express my joy."

A quiet moment at the CW Farm in Easton, Penn., c. 1937.

A CW retreat at the Easton Farm, c. 1945. Standing fourth from the left is Fr. Pacifique Roy, with Peter Maurin and Dorothy Day on either side.

Dorothy with Peter Maurin, a year before his death, reading the May 1948 issue of *The Catholic Worker.*

"Peter was the poor man of his day . . . He was impersonal in his love in that he loved all, saw all others around him as God saw them. In other words, he saw Christ in them."

"I found myself a barren woman, the joyful mother of children. It is not easy always to be joyful, to keep in mind the duty of delight."

Dorothy with grandchildren, late 1950s.

"Ammon was basically a romantic Irishman, and never lost that sense of drama, that love of life, tragic though its outcome so often was. He literally would have liked to give his life for the obliteration of wars and all injustice from the face of the earth."

Dorothy with grandchildren and Ammon Hennacy

Peter Maurin Farm, 1962.

Dorothy and Ammon picketing
in protest of compulsory Civil
Defense drills in New York City.

Dorothy with other demonstrators
under arrest.

Dorothy and Ammon court arrest in Washington Square Park by refusing to
take shelter in this 1956 drill.

*"We were, frankly, hoping for jail. Then we would not be running a house of
hospitality, we would not be dispensing food and clothing, we would not be
ministering to the destitute, but would be truly one with them."*

THE CATHOLIC WORKER

Vol. XXIX No. 1   JULY - AUGUST, 1962   Subscription: 25c Per Year   Price 1c

Torture In Spain

Norman Thomas and Salvador de Madariaga Urge Kennedy to Protest

The recent strikes in Spain and the meeting in Munich early in June of the Congress of the European Movement attended by opponents of the Franco regime such as Madariaga and Gil Robles have provoked numerous arrests, exilings and torture.

According to "IBERICA," a magazine devoted to the return of a democratic regime in Spain, liberal Catholics and trade unionists have been the principal victims of recent police repression in Spain.

More than one hundred workers and students are being tried on charges of belonging to the Popular Liberation Front and of having participated in the strikes.

In Valencia an army chaplain, Father Jose Bailo, has been tried by a military tribunal for the first time in Franco Spain. He was accused, in a trial, held behind closed doors, of distributing clandestine propaganda, insulting the Chief of State and inciting to disorder. The tribunal of three generals was headed by General Cabanillas, said to be a close

(Continued on page 2)

Exploitation In Our Hospitals

By EDGAR FORAND

There is probably no one group of workers in the city of New York who are any more exploited than the non-medical workers in our hospitals. These people, not to mention low wages and sometimes long hours, are even denied the right to representation of their own choosing and collective bargaining. About two-thirds of the workers are Negroes and Puerto Ricans who earn salaries from around $43 to $47 per week. After taxes and other deductions their net pay in many cases falls below $40 each week.

Although Governor Rockefeller stepped in to halt the strikes at two of the hospitals here, there are many problems ahead before the settlement is translated into real stability. The Governor said he would try to get the state law amended to grant collective bargaining rights to hitherto exempt hospital workers and would ask for a no-strike clause and compulsory arbitration in an impasse. A bill with similar purposes failed to get a vote last spring. It was violently opposed (according to the N. Y. Times) by powerful Roman Catholic leaders and leaders of other charitable institutions. The state labor federation swung against it at the end because of its arbitration proposal and penalty feature.

Of course, all this law will do is simply authorize unions to try to organize workers and win representation. The city went through a long, painful hospital strike three years ago. The central issue then, as now, was union recognition. The 1959 truce avoided the crux of the problem, which is how to prevent hospital strikes while at the same time giving the employees some effective means of improving their wretched conditions.

In the RWDSU Record for July 1, 1962, Charles Michaelson has focused his story on one individual; his job, his home, his life, his hopes and fears and things that make him risk the little he has in the effort to organize. This story, with minor changes, holds true for thousands of other voluntary hospital workers in N. Y. C.

Antonion Colon is 36 years old and a member of Drug and Hospital Employees Local 1199 of the RWDSU. Before he went out on strike he worked as a kitchenman —peeling vegetables, cleaning tables and the hospital's butcher shop, moving food carts from the kitchen to the employees' cafeteria

(Continued on page 8)

More About Cuba

By DOROTHY DAY

Last month the National Council of Catholic Men, with the consent of the Bishops of the United States, were making a documentary on the Catholic Worker movement, a week's work of filming to be condensed into a one-half hour of television time on a Sunday morning in this coming September on the program, Look Up and Live.

One of the questions asked of a group of the editors sitting in the third floor office on Chrystie Street was, "Do you agree with everything that is written in The Catholic Worker?"

As I remember it, all of them answered "No," and I would have given the same answer myself, if

I had been asked. But I was there just to introduce the others.

On another occasion the chancellor of the archdiocese of New York asked me if I saw everything that went into the Catholic Worker, for which after all I am responsible as editor and publisher. I told him yes, and that is true with few exceptions, when the paper was printed during my absence, and the material coming in late was used at once, assuming my approval. Perhaps on two or three occasions I disapproved of the emphasis given by the placing of material, as well as by the articles themselves. But no great harm was done.

Cardinal Hayes sent us word years ago, through Monsignor Chidwick that he approved our good work, and it was to be understood that we would make mistakes and the thing was not to persist in them. On another occasion Cardinal Spellman expressed approval of some of the aspects of our work, though it is undoubtedly true that there are many aspects of it which he is probably very dubious about, if not downright disapproving. The fact remains that we have been given, from the very first, the freedom which it is to be expected we laymen should take in handling temporal affairs, which after all is our province. That is a great gift. It seems to me that if the Catholic Worker did nothing else but indicate to critics the enormous freedom there is in the Church, which laymen so far have not taken advantage of, it is doing a good job.

A few months ago when I had a visit with Cardinal Leger in Montreal and he asked me about the position of the Catholic Worker in the church, I replied that we were a group of Catholics, engaged in writing and editing a paper dealing with the great problems of the day—the role of the State in man's life, war and peace, means and ends. That we had no chaplains, were in no way an organization included in Catholic Action, that we were under no bishop, and that we were therefore free to explore all possibilities of reform and restoration without committing the hierarchy to dangerous positions, and to try to rebuild the social order to make a better society" where it is easier for men to be good." To be good men, to be holy men is to be whole men, living a full life, developing all their capacities for good, using the talents God has given them.

The Cardinal had been looking at me from under his heavy brows, his deep set eyes scarcely visible. But when he lifted his head he smiled and commented, "St. John the Baptist."

We are among those who go ahead and prepare the way. This long preliminary is to indicate that we are Catholics in good standing, that we revere our clergy and are not hesitant to speak to the clergy. To print the criticism of others is not to mean that we are anticlerical. We are reporting events and the point of view which led to these events.

Of course we are not in agreement with the most basic and fundamental point of view as expressed by our friend Mario Gon-

(Continued on page 7)

Fritz Eichenberg

One Man At Hiroshima

By Elizabeth Sheehan

BURNING CONSCIENCE, by Claude Eatherly and Gunther Anders. Preface by Bertrand Russell. Monthly Review Press, New York, N.Y. $4.00.

"He who doesn't lose his mind over certain things has none to lose." —Lessing

"Hiroshima in itself is not enough to explain his behavior." —A Psychiatrist VA Hospital, Waco, Tex.

Between these two statements— one by an 18th century German writer and the other by a 20th century American doctor—lies a terrifying abyss.

It is bad enough to consider in the abstract this age in which man has learned to produce machinery,

the magnitude of whose effects staggers human mental, emotional and moral capacities. But we are not merely faced with an abstract issue. Condemned for life to this same abyss is a man who symbolizes in his unhappy self all that is implied in both the above sentences.

This man is Claude Eatherly, the "Hiroshima pilot," and this book brings to the American public for the first time a remarkable correspondence between Eatherly and the German philosopher, moralist and pacifist, Gunther Anders. These letters have already been widely circulated abroad, and in many countries, notably Japan, Eatherly has long since been recognized as a victim of the mental and moral effects of the atomic

age. In America, however, this disturbed and disturbing "war hero" has proved a thorny embarrassment to family, friends, law enforcement officials, and the United States Air Force. So few of us here even know who he is!

Claude Robert Eatherly was the 26 year old Air Force Major from Van Alstyne, Texas, chosen to pilot the lead plane over Hiroshima early on the morning of August 6, 1945. A veteran of many conventional Pacific bombing missions, Eatherly gave the coded "go-ahead" signal to the bomb-carrying plane, thus loosing physical death upon a city and moral, if not also physical death upon the world.

Flying his B-29 Straight Flush back to the island base at Tinian

(Continued on page 6)

RESPECT FOR LIFE

Ammon Hennacy is fasting for forty days, as penance for our dropping the first atom bomb on Hiroshima. In the ordinary course of events he would be fasting seventeen days this year, since seventeen years have passed since the dropping of the bomb. But he is including in his fast all of the proposed executions, a plea for a young man whose execution is slated for September 14 and for two other young men condemned to death in Utah where the death penalty is a choice of shooting or hanging. Ammon is running the Joe Hill House of Hospitality and St. Joseph's refuge at 72½ Postoffice Place, Salt Lake City. He will send you his leaflets on request.

July-August 1962 issue of the *Catholic Worker* features a wood engraving by Quaker artist Fritz Eichenberg.

"Hard though it was, it was but a token fast, considering the problems of the world we live in . . . May we try harder to do more in the future."

Dorothy with Lanza del Vasto in Rome, where she joined a group of women fasting for ten days during the last session of Vatican II.

Collection of Jim Forest

Collection of Jim Forest

In 1965, about to address an anti-war rally in Union Square, where Tom Cornell and others burned their draft cards. (Dorothy is being assisted by Jim Forest.)

Dorothy in Red Square during her visit to the Soviet Union in 1971.

Catholic Worker Archives

"What can we do? We can pray. We can pray without ceasing, as St. Paul said."

"Remember the boycott and help the strikers . . . Their struggle has gone on for years now. It is the first breakthrough to achieve some measure of justice for these poorest and most beloved of God's children."

In 1973, picketing with the United Farm Workers in California. Dorothy was subsequently arrested.

A visit by Mother Teresa at the Maryhouse office in 1979.

"We cannot love God unless we love each other. We know Him in the breaking of bread, and we know each other in the breaking of bread, and we are not alone anymore."

On the beach in Staten Island.

Dorothy Day's grave on Staten Island.

DOROTHY DAY
NOVEMBER 8, 1897 — NOVEMBER 29, 1980
DEO GRATIAS

ized not by Christians but by Communists and that the differences between the two groups were such that as yet she had no deep friendships with Catholics and no real welcome from radicals. She had a religious faith and a social conscience but no community. She could only watch and admire those campaigning for social justice. "I could not be out there with them."

She felt useless. "How little, how puny my work had been since becoming a Catholic, I thought. How self-centered, how ingrown, how lacking in sense of community! My summer of quiet reading and prayer, my self-absorption seemed sinful as I watched my brothers in their struggle, not for themselves but for others. How our dear Lord must love them, I kept thinking to myself. They were His friends, His comrades, and who knows how close to His heart in their attempt to work for justice. I remembered our Lord overthrowing the money-changers' tables in the temple. . . . [What] divine courage on the part of this obscure Jew, going into the temple and with bold scorn for all the riches of this world, scattering the coins and the traffickers' gold."

The banners passed, and the battered marchers disbanded peaceably, no doubt wondering who was changed or what structures of life might be improved by their appeal.

Dorothy returned to a hotel room to write down her impressions and then went to church to pray.

December 8 was a major holy day for Catholics, the feast of the Immaculate Conception, celebrating a special grace that had touched Mary's life even from the moment of her conception in her mother's womb. Dorothy went to a church built to commemorate the event, the National Shrine of the Immaculate Conception at Catholic University. The upper church was still under construction. She went into the crypt beneath, with its low vaulted ceilings and dark chapels lit with the flickering of vigil candles.

"There I offered up a special prayer, a prayer which came with tears and anguish, that some way would open up for me to use what talents I possessed for my fellow workers, for the poor."

A Penny a Copy

Dorothy returned to New York eager to be with Tamar and to share news of the Hunger March with her brother John and his wife, Tessa, with whom she was sharing her apartment at the time. All were at home, but there was a stranger waiting for her as well. His shabby suit and tie bore the wrinkles of having been slept in and his face seemed as weather-beaten as his clothing. Yet he wasn't down-and-out in his welcoming smile or in the warmth of his grey eyes. These communicated gentleness, vitality and intellectual energy, and when he spoke, his calloused hands were as lively as his thought. Altogether, he could easily have been among the marchers Dorothy had so admired in Washington.

"I am Peter Maurin," he said in a thick French accent. "George Shuster, editor of *The Commonweal*, told me to look you up. Also, a red-haired Irish Communist in Union Square told me to see you. He says we think alike."

On their first encounter, Dorothy was tired from her travel and wanted to focus on family needs rather than talk with an unexpected visitor. After a brief conversation, she suggested Peter return another time.

He was back the next day, animated with his plan to provide Dorothy with an entirely new education. Perhaps more remarkable than the providence of their meeting was Dorothy's willingness to listen. To many others, he would have seemed just one more street-corner prophet. New York had many. Yet Dorothy gave him not only patient but increasingly appreciative attention. He wanted her to look at history in a new way which centered not on the rise and fall of empires but rather on the lives of the saints. He was certain that sanctity was at the center of what really mattered, and that any program of social change must emphasize sanctity and community.

Peter had been praying for a collaborator and was certain Dorothy was the answer to his prayers. Her articles and what others had told him about her, as well as his own immediate impressions, convinced him that Dorothy was a new St. Catherine of Siena, the medieval reformer and peace negotiator who had counseled and reprimanded both popes and princes. What Saint Catherine had done in the fourteenth century, Peter believed Dorothy could do in the twentieth. She would "move mountains, and have influence on governments, temporal and spiritual."

While Peter was tireless in expounding his vision and philosophy, he was hesitant to talk about himself. Only slowly did Dorothy piece together some of the main facts of Peter's life.

He had been born into a family of peasant farmers in the south of France in 1877, the eldest of twenty-two children. At sixteen he entered a Catholic teaching order, the Christian Brothers, with whom he remained nine years. In 1902, he left the order and became active in *Le Sillon* (The Furrow), a movement which advocated Christian democracy and supported cooperatives and unions. But in 1908, as *Le Sillon* shifted from its early religious basis toward secular politics, Peter withdrew and soon after joined the stream of emigrants who were leaving France for Canada, where there was no military conscription and land was cheap. For two years, until his partner died, he homesteaded in Saskatchewan, then took whatever work he could find, first in Canada and then in the United States. By the time he met Dorothy, he had quarried stone, dug irrigation ditches, harvested wheat, cut lumber and laid railway tracks. He had worked in brickyards, steel mills and coal mines. He had been jailed for vagrancy and for traveling unticketed on freight cars. He had traded French lessons for his simple needs. He had never married. For five years, he had been the handyman at a Catholic boys' camp in upstate New York, receiving meals, use of the chaplain's library, living space in the barn (shared with a horse), and pocket money as needed.

During his years of wandering and hard labor, he had come to a Franciscan attitude toward both property and money: he had nearly none of either and rejoiced in poverty as if it were his bride. His unencumbered life offered ample time for both study and prayer, out of which a vision had taken form of a social order "in which it would be easier for men to be good." As often as his work allowed, he made his way to New York City. A "flop house" hotel on the Bowery provided austere lodging for forty cents a night. His days were spent either at the New York Public Library or in expounding his ideas — often at Union Square — to anyone who showed a flicker of interest. After all, he reasoned, the way to reach the man on the street is to be on the street. No doubt his accent and threadbare suit convinced many that there was no need to listen. But Peter was a born teacher, lively and good humored, and often enough he found willing listeners — not only hobos and radicals with time on their hands, but professors and bankers. One friendly listener was the editor and educator, George Shuster of *Commonweal*, who told Peter about Dorothy and gave him her address on East 15th Street.

"There is no revolution without a theory of revolution," Peter told Dorothy, quoting Lenin, but what is needed, he went on, is not a bloody Red Revolution, built on mountains of casualties, but a peaceful Green Revolution. For the theory of a Green Revolution to be made known and put into practice, a journal was needed, a radical Catholic paper that would publicize Catholic social teaching and promote the steps that could bring about the peaceful transformation of society "building a new society within the shell of the old." Dorothy, he said, should be the editor of such a publication.

Start a radical Catholic newspaper! It seemed to Dorothy that if family roots, life experience and religious conviction had prepared her for anything, it was just such a task. It was obvious that the few Catholic publications willing to publish her writings had no revolutionary vision and weren't reaching the down-and-out.

"But how are we to start it?"

"I enunciate the principles," Peter declared.

"But where do we get the money?"

"In the history of the saints," Peter answered, "capital is raised by prayer. God sends you what you need when you need it. You will be able to pay the printer. Just read the lives of the saints."

Dorothy had only recently read *Sorrow Built a Bridge*, a biography of Rose Hawthorne Lathrop, a convert to Catholicism who had abandoned her social position, rented a three-room tenement flat on the Lower East Side in New York, and opened its doors to penniless neighbors who were dying of cancer. From her hospitality to the terminally ill had sprung a religious order that still operates hospices for the indigent dying in several cities.

"Why not start a newspaper in the same way?" Dorothy asked herself. "I began to look on my kitchen as an editorial office, my brother as an assistant to write heads and to help with mechanical make-up. Tamar and I could go out to sell papers on the streets!"

The Paulist Press was willing to set type and print 2,500 copies of an eight-page tabloid paper for $57. Dorothy calculated she could pay this with recent income from her writing and research work and by delaying the payment of her utility bills.

"We would sell the paper, I decided, for a cent a copy, to make it so cheap that anyone could afford to buy." She plunged into writing the first issue, preparing articles on labor, strikes and unemployment. Her own writing retained its usual highly personal style. In addition she selected six of Peter's "Easy Essays," as her brother John had christened them. These were an orator's blend of manifesto and poetry. One of them included in the first issue protested the crippling grip of wealth on the Church:

> Christ drove the money changers
> out of the Temple.
> But today nobody dares
> to drive the money lenders
> out of the Temple.
> And nobody dares
> to drive the money lenders
> out of the Temple
> because the money lenders

> have taken a mortgage
> on the Temple.

The name Peter had proposed for the paper was *The Catholic Radical.* Radical, he pointed out, came from the Latin word, *radix,* for root. The radical is someone who doesn't settle for cosmetic solutions, but goes to the root of personal and social problems.

Dorothy felt that the name should refer to the class of its readers rather than the attitude of its editors and so chose to name it *The Catholic Worker* instead.

"Man proposes and woman disposes," Peter responded meekly.

On May 1, the radicals and workers who crowded Union Square to celebrate their revolutionary hopes were the recipients of the first issue.

Everyone's Paper

Peter Maurin's name — misspelled Maurain — had been listed with Dorothy's as an editor. But he wasn't among those distributing the new paper at Union Square. Apart from his own Easy Essays, which filled several columns, he found *The Catholic Worker* a painful disappointment and had no desire to be considered co-responsible. "It's everyone's paper," he said woefully after looking at the first issue. "And everyone's paper is no one's paper." He quietly left Dorothy's apartment, where he had been a daily visitor for months, and weeks passed before she saw him again.

Dorothy was so caught up with the needs of the infant paper that she hardly noticed his absence. Mailing out sample copies to friends and editors, writing hurried appeals begging for support, she must have been relieved to be momentarily without Peter's tireless instruction. The most pressing problem was the lack of money. If help wasn't found quickly, the first issue would be the last. Dorothy made the rather spectacular sacrifice, for a writer, of pawning her own typewriter. Fortunately, enthusiastic letters began to arrive, each with a subscription order and many with additional contributions. The typewriter was recovered from the pawn shop and Peter returned. He had recovered from his initial disappointment and was ready to resume Dorothy's instruction in radical Christianity. He arrived daily at three in the afternoon and often stayed until eleven at night, making his "points," while Dorothy and others in the household carried on with their chores and the care of Tamar.

It became clear that his objection to the first issue wasn't simply that Dorothy's presence rather than his own dominated its pages. Peter was remarkably free of the need for personal recognition, and he admired Dorothy's writing. What he found missing in much of the paper were the ideas and principles, the strategy for a new social order, which he had hoped the paper would communicate page after page. He felt that Dorothy hadn't really understood what he had been saying all those weeks. If the first issue were pruned of his own contribution and the occasional quotations from the Bible and papal encyclicals, most of the surviving material could have been published in any journal commonly distributed on Union Square. There were stories about strikes, trials, racism, child labor and economic exploitation. The first *Catholic Worker* to a large extent was simply one

more journal of radical protest, different from others only because it was
edited by Catholics rather than Marxists.

Peter was a peculiar radical. He had little interest in protest, which he
believed could do little to bring about real change. The old order would
die from neglect rather than criticism. What was needed first of all, he was
convinced, was a vision of a future society, and with this a program of
constructive steps with which to begin realizing bits of the vision in one's
own life.

"Strikes don't strike me," Peter said. But they struck Dorothy. She was
heart and soul with strikers and protesters. Peter saw no point in struggling
for better hours or higher pay in places where the work was dehumanizing.
He considered assembly lines to be as brutalizing as prisons and said it was
time to "fire the bosses"—to leave behind time clocks and shift labor. But
where, Dorothy and others asked, could they go? How would they live?
"There is no unemployment on the land," Peter replied. *The Catholic
Worker* should stand for a decentralized society, a society of cooperation
rather than coercion, with artisans and craftsmen, with small factories that
were worker-owned and worker-run. Coming together in agricultural communities, worker and scholar could both sweat and think together and
develop "a worker-scholar synthesis." *The Catholic Worker* should be vision-
ary. It should convince its readers not just to complain or to denounce but
to take up the work of building "a new society within the shell of the old,"
a society in which it would be "easier for man to be good." All this was, of
course, utopian. The word was often hurled at Peter as if no other response
was necessary. Peter was accused of being a romantic. He was longing,
critics said, for the medieval past rather than for the industrial future. But
Peter believed that capitalist and communist had more in common than
they liked to admit: both were looking with a common eye toward a horizon
of smokestacks. Both communist and anti-communist were generally town
people, few of whom aspired to the plow, the chicken coop, the 6 A.M.
milking, the midnight calving, and the 365-day work year that the care of
livestock requires.

Yet following Peter's return, Dorothy became more open to his critique
of assembly-line civilization. Surely there must be something more to struggle for than improved, unionized industrialism. Surely community was better than mass society. Surely it was better to grow up with space, air and
land. Surely life on the land wasn't just for our ancestors. And would not
a land-centered society provide a better base for a way of life that centered
in faith? Surely others too were longing for a society rooted in faith, hope
and love.

Yet her way and Peter's were different, a difference Dorothy attributed
in part to what she saw as a fundamental difference between man and
woman. Men, Dorothy felt, tended to preoccupation with the future and
were generally more abstract, while women were rooted in the present and
were involved with solving immediate practical problems. Drawing on her

own experience, she felt that "woman is saved by child bearing" which imposes on her "a rule of life which involves others" and through which "she will be saved in spite of herself." Men didn't have to be so anchored. "Women think with their whole bodies. More than men do, women see things as a whole."

With the second issue of *The Catholic Worker*, Peter withdrew his name as an editor and announced that henceforth he was responsible only for what he signed himself. Yet from that issue onward, the paper as a whole, including Dorothy's own writing, bore greater evidence of Peter's influence. This wasn't, however, at the expense of Dorothy's preoccupation with the here and now. She continued to identify with anyone who was protesting injustice and struggling even for slight improvements in the social order. She continued to side with strikers and union organizers and to approve of much that the Left was doing, even if it never questioned urbanization or industrialism. But she found ways to articulate a hope for the future that had fewer smokestacks and smaller cities.

In the second issue Peter described his program in more detail: his call for discussion and study groups and for the foundation of houses of hospitality and farming communes. In essence, it was a call, he cheerfully admitted, for Christian communism. "I am not afraid of the word communism," he wrote, but it was not something to be imposed. "I am not saying that my program is for everyone. It is for those who choose to embrace it."

Readers were invited by Peter to the first "round-table discussion," an image suggesting a gathering in which all who take part have equal standing. A $3 deposit had already been paid for a large hall on East 4th Street, he announced to his readers. He must have been disappointed when rather few people showed up on the appointed day—about fifteen. (Even so, an enduring Catholic Worker tradition began. Hardly a week has passed since then without a weekly public meeting at the New York Catholic Worker, and the practice is followed by many other Catholic Worker communities.)

By the fall, it was clear that the new paper was meeting a real need. Few papers have experienced such rapid growth as did *The Catholic Worker* in its first year. Within a few months the number of copies printed rose from 2,500 to 75,000, though much of the printing was to fill bulk orders rather than subscriptions. Readers found a voice in *The Catholic Worker* that was unique among both religious and political journals, with a special intimacy and at-homeness. There were principles and news, but much of the paper was written as if it were a letter between friends. It had had deep roots in a specific city and neighborhood and was full of local smells, sounds and small events that national papers ignored.

"Late Fall is here," Dorothy wrote in the November issue. "A haze hangs over the city. Fog rises on the river, and the melancholy note of the river boats is heard at night. The leaves are dropping from the fig tree in the back yard. There is the smell of chestnuts in the air, but if you buy the chestnuts, most of them are wormy. It is better to make popcorn over the fire at night. For we have fires now. The kettle sings on the range of the kitchen (the range cost eight dollars second-hand and doesn't burn much coal), and visitors to *The Catholic Worker* office are drinking much tea and coffee. . . . And there is the smell of grapes in the air—rich, luscious Concord grapes."

Yet her attention was never held entirely by her own hearth. Against this background of good smells and warm fires, she described the daily tragedies of her neighbors. Winter was beginning and evictions were increasing. "People come in to ask for winter clothes and for help in finding apartments where relief checks will be accepted."

Ambassadors of God

The October 1933 *Catholic Worker* included an "Easy Essay" by Peter on houses of hospitality:

> People who are in need
> and are not afraid to beg
> give to people not in need
> the occasion to do good
> for goodness' sake.
> Modern society calls the beggar
> bum and panhandler and gives him the bum's rush.
> But the Greeks used to say
> that people in need
> are ambassadors of the gods.
> Although you may be called
> bums and panhandlers
> you are in fact the ambassadors of God.
> As God's ambassadors
> you should be given
> food, clothing and shelter
> by those who are able to give it.
> Mohammedan teachers tell us
> that God commands hospitality.
> And hospitality is still practiced
> in Mohammedan countries. But the duty of hospitality
> is neither taught nor practiced
> in Christian countries.

Peter's study of Church history had shown him that in earlier times hospitality had been both taught and practiced by Christians. He was delighted to discover that a Church council in the fifth century had obliged bishops to establish houses of hospitality in connection with each parish church. These were open to the poor, the sick, the orphaned, the old, the traveler and pilgrim, and the needy of every kind. Such houses were a response to Jesus' identification of himself with the homeless: "I was a stranger and you took me in." The old hospice tradition was still practiced by monasteries, but urgently needed revival in rank-and-file Christianity. In fact, Peter realized, houses of hospitality could not only serve as places of friendly shelter but also could provide reading rooms and vocational training and be centers of prayer, discussion, and study. Parishes should sponsor such houses and regard them as essential to parish life. "We need Parish Homes as well as Parish Domes," Peter said. He resisted the thought that lay Christians should welcome only their friends and leave care of strangers to hired professionals. The works of love and mercy were for everyone and should be regarded as the ordinary Christian way of life. Every home should have its "Christ Room" open to receive the ambassadors of God. Each of us should be ready to recognize Christ in an unfamiliar face. "What you did to the least person," said Jesus, "you did to me."

Self-giving love, Peter stressed, was the constant witness of the early Church. At a personal sacrifice the hungry were fed, the naked were clothed, the homeless were sheltered, and the suffering were cared for. Those without faith who noticed these things were astonished and said, "See how they love each other." But in our own day, Peter wrote,

> the poor are no longer
> fed, clothed and sheltered
> at a personal sacrifice
> but at the expense of the taxpayers.
> And because the poor
> are no longer
> fed, clothed and sheltered
> at a personal sacrifice
> the pagans say about the Christians,
> "See how they pass the buck."

Surrounded by people in need, and attracting volunteers who were excited about the ideas they discovered in *The Catholic Worker*, it was inevitable that the editors would soon be given the chance to put their editorials into practice. Dorothy's 15th Street apartment was itself the seed of many houses of hospitality to come. Its door was open from early morning until late at night. Anyone was welcome. There was, Dorothy recalled, "ever-flowing coffee" and for much of the day "mulligan stew"—a stew of whatever was at hand—simmered on the cast-iron stove. By the wintertime, a nearby apartment was rented with space in it for ten women. Soon after a place for men was rented on 7th Street behind St. Brigid's Church. A priest told Dorothy about an old house on Charles Street in Greenwich Village that was empty and for rent, with room enough for staff and guests to live in the same building, and with space for an office and a free clothing room. Money was coming in steadily. (By December, there were 100,000 copies being printed each month.) But what seemed huge in 1934 was far too cramped a place by 1936. The community moved into two buildings, one in front of the other, on Mott Street in Chinatown. Without delay, the hungry and lonely found their way. Lines formed. No enlargement of the Catholic Worker could possibly find room for all those in need of a bowl of soup, a piece of bread, a cup of coffee. Mainly they were men, Dorothy wrote, "grey men, the color of lifeless trees and bushes and winter soil, who had in them as yet none of the green of hope, the rising sap of faith." An atmosphere of helpless resentment hung over them which occasionally exploded in furious fights on the line. They came and went, most of them anonymous. Perhaps they were surprised that, in contrast with a number of centers of Christian inspiration, at the Catholic Worker no one preached at them. A crucifix on the wall was the only unmistakable evidence of the faith of those who were welcoming them — a staff of volunteers who received no salary, only food, board and occasionally a bit of pocket money.

Those who came regularly came to be known by name — often just the first name and an adjective: Smokey Joe, Italian Mike, St. Louis Marie, Mad Paul, Alabama Andy. They began to see the Catholic Worker as home, taking possession of some daily chore, a particular chair or corner, and sometimes their own bed.

The house most often heard about in *The Catholic Worker* was St. Joseph's in New York, but by the time the community moved to Mott Street in 1936, Dorothy was already in touch with thirty-three other Catholic Worker houses spread across the country. Due to the Depression, there were plenty of people needing them. The New York house alone was feeding four hundred people a day in 1937, and a year later twice that number, a seemingly endless line of discarded people. Most of the food they were served was either begged or given. Much of the food was past selling: day-old bread or vegetables and fruit going rotten. Those who prepared the meals threw out what they wouldn't eat themselves and found ways to make good use of the rest. Even rock-hard bread makes excellent bread pudding. And occasionally the meal was made from first-class ingredients — a gift from a rectory or convent or sympathetic food merchant. In later years a visitor to the Catholic Worker one day asked a member of the staff — Tom Cornell — if there was any standard to be applied in accepting free food. "Of course," said Tom. "Nothing but the best, and the best is none too good for God's poor." Certainly this had been Dorothy's view from the Catholic Worker's first days: "What a delightful thing it is," she wrote in the 1930s, "to be boldly profligate, to ignore the price of coffee and to go on serving good coffee and the finest bread to the long line of destitute who come to us."

From time to time Dorothy was able to set a stunning example of giving away what was given to the Catholic Worker. Another story told by Tom Cornell recalls a well-dressed woman who visited the Worker house one day and gave Dorothy a diamond ring. Dorothy thanked the visitor, slipped the ring in her pocket, and later in the day gave it to an old woman who lived alone and often ate her meals at St. Joseph's. One of the staff protested to Dorothy that the ring could better have been sold at the Diamond Exchange and the money used to pay the woman's rent for a year. Dorothy replied that the woman had her dignity and could do as she liked with the ring. She could sell it for rent money or take a trip to the Bahamas. Or she could enjoy having a diamond ring on her hand just like the woman who had brought it to the Worker. "Do you suppose," Dorothy asked, "that God created diamonds only for the rich?"

Dorothy's attitude toward those who came to the Catholic Worker was often criticized. She wasn't helping the "deserving poor," it was said, but rather drunkards, loafers and thieves. Why were there no employment or rehabilitation programs? Didn't she realize that the clothes that the Worker gave away were often sold or bartered for drink? Anyway, didn't Jesus himself say that the poor would be with us always? "Yes," Dorothy replied again and again, "but we are not content that there should be so many of them. The class structure is *our* making and by *our* consent, not God's, and we must do what we can to change it. We are urging revolutionary change."

A social worker asked Dorothy one day how long the down-and-out were permitted to stay at the Worker. "We let them stay forever," Dorothy answered. "They live with us, they die with us, and we give them a Christian burial. We pray for them after they are dead. Once they are taken in, they become members of the family. Or rather they always were members of the family. They are our brothers and sisters in Christ."

To the Land!

At the heart of Peter's program was the "Green Revolution" through which he hoped society would become recentered on the farm. Though Dorothy was far more city-centered than Peter, she hadn't given up her rural beach house. She knew how brutalizing the inner city could be and respected her need for space and quiet. Ferry rides to Staten Island and long walks at the edge of the sea renewed her. She could name all the local wildflowers and was a devoted gardener. Peter's proposal of farming communities had a powerful appeal for her. She envisioned what a Catholic Worker farm might be: a group of families whose buildings centered on a chapel, sharing daily Mass, all subject to one another and accepting the authority of an abbot-like coordinator.

The first "farm," rented in 1935, was a twelve-room house with a garden not far from her beach house. Dorothy afterward remembered it as a "household of sad afflicted creatures." The short-lived experiment was succeeded by a more ambitious foundation in Pennsylvania, an old ten-acre farm on a hilltop in Easton, seventy-five miles west of New York. The sum of $1,250 bought the land, a rundown house, a rutted dirt road and a small stand of aged fruit trees. Later a second farm was purchased further down the hillside. The Worker's base at Easton was a spot, Dorothy found, "of unutterable beauty." Yet community life at Mary Farm, as it was named, proved often difficult and sometimes grim. "Eat what you raise and raise what you eat," said Peter Maurin, who came to live at Mary Farm. Unfortunately there were always more people interested in eating food than raising it, who preferred a discussion of theology or politics to care of the fields or repair of a hinge.

"It seemed," Dorothy wrote, "that the more people there were around, the less got done." Small matters took on huge and divisive significance. Physical battle exploded one day following the disappearance of an egg one resident had set aside for lunch. Peter, who witnessed the fight, responded with a Gandhi-like vow to do without eggs and milk for the rest of the summer, thus shaming the combatants into a brief truce. His act of self-denial animated a debate within the community as to whether justice came before love. "Those holding the view that justice came first," Dorothy observed, "were the most avid to get their share of everything, and the last to practice self-denial." While arguments flared, invisible walls rose within the community. Peter alone seemed to look after such chores as mending the road, collecting the garbage, and repairing the fences.

A split developed between the upper and lower farms. In the upper farm the men governed their families with a strict insistence on obedience, certain that it was man's God-given role to rule over women as judges, and that it fell to women to hew the wood, draw the water, till the field and clothe the family. "Women were forbidden to speak unless spoken to," Dorothy reported, "and were compelled to knock on the doors of even their own kitchens and dining rooms if there were men present." The men of the upper farm considered themselves "the true Catholic Workers" in contrast to Dorothy and Peter and all those associated with the lower farm.

Dorothy never lived at Easton, though she often visited. Despite the many problems she encountered even at the lower farm—problems often quite similar to those found in Worker houses in the cities—she managed to find much needed refreshment: peaceful meals, good discussions, quiet hours of prayer, even times of forgiveness and reconciliation. One evening Dorothy wrote of the breeze sighing in the apple trees while moonlight made the fields look as if they had been washed. "There was a quiet and perfect peace and a happiness so deep and strong and thankful that even my words of prayer seemed inadequate to express my joy."

More precious than the rare moments of quiet and beauty were those visitors who seemed to bring a special grace and mystery to the table. Years later Dorothy still recalled an early guest, a Jewish worker from the Lower East Side who wore a rosary around his neck and who recited the Psalms in Hebrew. "He had the gentleness of St. Francis," she wrote. He helped in the garden, walking on the earth in his bare feet. "I can feel things growing," he said. "I look at the little plants, and I draw them up out of the earth with the power of love in my eyes." One day he sat at the table and held in his hands a piece of dark rye bread from a kosher bakery. "It is the black bread of the poor," he said. "It is Russian Jewish bread. It is the flesh of Lenin. Lenin held bread up to the people and he said, 'This is my body, broken for you.' So they worship Lenin. He brought them bread." Some at the table were shocked at what they judged a blasphemy, but Dorothy felt blessed. Yes, perhaps he was mad, but she often found it easier to see Christ in such madness than to see it in the sane, the doctrinaire, the rigid. The sane ones rarely felt life in the earth and insisted that bread carry only the correct passenger.

As happened repeatedly with Catholic Worker farms, the one at Easton had to be given up. Whatever joys it brought, its particular problems proved insoluble. Many who had come to spend the rest of their lives in community left after the first frost, discovering, Dorothy noted, "the reason for cities and relief roles." Those who remained were often the most difficult to live with. In 1946 the lower farm was sold to local people; in 1949 the upper farm was deeded to "the true Catholic Workers" who were offering the world a model of patriarchal order.

It seemed an awful failure, and indeed was, yet there were consolations. "We might not have established a model community," said Dorothy, "but many a family got a vacation, many a sick person was nursed back to health, crowds of slum children had the run of the woods and fields for weeks, and groups of students spent happy hours discussing the green revolution."

Even then the hope of community on the land was not abandoned. Another farm was purchased in upstate New York near Newburgh. Called the Maryfarm Retreat House, it was destined for a longer life, though here again there were heated battles for the flag of orthodoxy and families who became pitted against each other. It was through such experiences that Dorothy reluctantly came to see that the responsibility of the Catholic Worker was not so much to found model communities, with families gathered peacefully around a chapel, but rather to provide a certain service to the poor and occasionally to those who were mentally destitute or broken. She came to see the farms more as rural houses of hospitality for some of those who had found their way to the Catholic Worker through the soup line. At the same time, the farms could be used for group or private retreats. "We aimed high, too high," said Dorothy. "But at least we were able, as Peter said, 'to arouse the conscience.'"

The Works of Mercy versus

the Works of War

Jesus healed many and killed no one. The last healing miracle he worked was on behalf of one of the men arresting him, injured by a sword blow Peter had inflicted while attempting to defend Jesus. Jesus turned toward his friend with the sharp command, "Put away your sword, for whoever lives by the sword shall perish by the sword." For several centuries Christians understood that Jesus was not only speaking to Peter at that moment but to anyone who was following him. Christians died in Roman arenas by the thousands without defending themselves. Some were condemned to death specifically for their refusal to do military service. "I will not be a soldier of this world," St. Maximilian told the Roman proconsul during a brief trial, "for I am a soldier of Christ." He died saying to his executioners, "Christ lives!"

The Church Dorothy Day had joined had accommodated itself to empire and war many centuries before, beginning in the time of Constantine. Popes had commanded armies and declared holy wars. Life without weapons, the early practice of Christians, had become the peculiar witness of those in religious orders, while ordinary men were expected to take up arms when those in political authority ordered them to war. St. Francis had attempted to revive the pacifist way in the thirteenth century. Several post-Reformation "peace churches" — the Mennonites, Quakers and Brethren — refused any military role, but by the twentieth century, it was unknown for Catholics to take such a position. On the contrary, in every country they could be relied on by the military, perhaps in no country so willingly as in the United States. American Catholics, so long accused of being more loyal to Rome than to Washington, had excelled in patriotism. Carved over the entrance to countless Catholic schools was the Latin motto, *"Pro Deo et Patria"* — for God and country. The American flag stood near the altar in the sanctuary.

Attentive readers of *The Catholic Worker* in 1935 must have been surprised to discover in the March issue a dialogue written by Father Paul Hanly Furfey between an imaginary patriot and Christ. The patriot, who could have been almost any American Catholic, said that he loved peace as much as anyone, but he was a realist. "A strong system of national defense is our best assurance of peace. National defense is the patriotic duty of every American citizen."

"All that take the sword shall perish by the sword," Jesus responded.

"Yet," the patriot pointed out, "we must be practical! After all, Japan and Russia are casting jealous eyes at us. Our basic policies conflict. We must arm ourselves against such nations."

"You have heard that it has been said," Christ replied, "that you shall love your neighbor and hate your enemy. But I say to you, love your enemies, do good to them that hate you, and pray for those who persecute and slander you."

"A noble doctrine!" answered the patriot. "Even so, common sense obliges us to be prepared to defend our own territory."

"To him that strikes you on the one cheek, offer the other as well," said Jesus. "Of him who takes away your goods, ask not for their return."

"But national defense," said the patriot, "isn't only to defend material rights, but is a question of life and death. Only a strong system of national defense will guarantee our personal security."

"Be not afraid of those who kill the body and after that have no more that they can do."

"But there is such a thing as a just war," argued the patriot, recalling familiar Church teaching. "Under certain circumstances a nation has a right to declare war."

"You have heard that it has been said," Christ replied, "an eye for an eye and a tooth for a tooth, but I say to you not to resist evil."

Publication of the dialogue was the first clear indication in *The Catholic Worker* of Dorothy's conviction that following Jesus required the renunciation of hatred and killing. From its third year, the paper increasingly voiced this unfamiliar position, which many Catholics found shocking and possibly heretical. Dorothy described herself and the paper she edited as "pacifist," from the Latin for peacemaker, with the implication that genuine, lasting peace is made only by peaceful means.

In the summer of 1936, with the outbreak of the Spanish Civil War, Dorothy's pacifism was tested against the reality of a war in which radicals and fascists were opposing each other, and in which the fascist side, led by Franco, presented itself as defender of the Catholic faith. Nearly every bishop and Catholic publication rallied behind Franco, considering only that he was anti-Communist and pro-Catholic. *The Catholic Worker* refused to support either side in the war and actively challenged Catholics in their identification with Franco. Before backing him, Dorothy wrote, one should "take another look at recent events in Germany to see how much love the Catholic Church can expect" from fascists. One of Catholicism's great philosophers, Jacques Maritain, published an essay in *The Catholic Worker* warning of the anti-Semitism that was characteristic of fascism, whether

Spanish or German, "a certain religious racism" such as had earlier driven European Christians to murder and terrify so many Jews. Dorothy felt a similar worry for the Jews, reminding *Worker* readers that they were "the race that Christ was part of." Peter wrote that the Jews were an "exceptional, unique and imperishable people which is protected by God, preserved as the apple of his eye."

Furious letters poured into *The Catholic Worker* office. Did Dorothy not know that nuns were being raped and priests shot, that churches were being razed by Spanish communists and anarchists, and that only Franco could defend the Church from complete destruction?

"We all know," Dorothy replied in an editorial, "that there is frightful persecution of religion in Spain. . . . [Even so] we are opposed to the use of force as a means of settling personal, national or international disputes." Yes, there have been many priests and nuns who were martyrs of the Church. But do we honor them by taking up in their name the weapons they refused to use? To kill for those who had chosen vocations excluding all violence "would be martyrdom wasted and blood spilled in vain." Could Christians dare to make the way of Christ and his cross their own? "Today the whole world is in the midst of revolution. We are living through it now— all of us. And frankly, we are calling for Saints." We ourselves, she continued, must be as ready as those priests and nuns in Spain to suffer or die in unarmed witness to our faith. "There must be a disarmament of the heart." Only then can our love and prayer have the strength to overcome evil.

While *The Catholic Worker*'s position was vindicated in later years, at the time it cost the young paper much of its support. Many individual subscriptions and most of the bundle orders were canceled. In several dioceses, bishops banned the paper from every church and parish school. *The Catholic Worker* was printing 160,000 copies a month when the war began. At the end the number was barely 50,000.

The Spanish war ended with a fascist victory in March, 1939. In September world war began with the German invasion of Poland, though U.S. entry into the war occurred only two years later.

Anti-Semitism became increasingly apparent not only in Europe but in the United States, and not least in the Catholic Church. America's most famous anti-Semite was a priest, Father Charles Coughlin, arch-foe of President Roosevelt's "New Deal" and editor of *Social Justice* magazine. A coast-to-coast audience of millions faithfully listened to a weekly radio program on which Coughlin ranted against Roosevelt, Jews and the Communists. In his view, rich banking Jews and poor Communist Jews, however opposed they seemed, were taking control of the world in a joint Jewish conspiracy. Those selling the Coughlin paper on the streets in New York shouted "Communist" at their *Catholic Worker* counterparts, sometimes tearing the paper from their hands or even knocking them down.

In May 1939 Dorothy was among the founders of the Committee of

Catholics To Fight Anti-Semitism, which launched a new paper, *The Voice*, to counter Coughlin's publication. *The Voice* lasted until the U.S. entry into the war, when sympathy for the Jews finally seemed to outweigh anti-Semitism.

The Catholic Worker's pacifism did not put the movement in the camp of neutralism. Opposition to Hitler led the New York Catholic Worker community to the docks on the Upper West Side in 1935 to join in picketing the German liner *Bremen*. One of the demonstrators was shot in the leg by a guard on board the ship when the demonstrator climbed a mast in the attempt to remove the swastika flag. "We fled down the street afterward," Dorothy recalled, "together with other protesters, to escape a squad of police, and witnessed some police brutality which we later protested against." On other occasions, the Catholic Worker joined in picketing the German embassy. An appeal published in *The Catholic Worker* called on the nation to open its doors to "all Jews who wish free access to American hospitality." Similar appeals came from many quarters, but went largely unheeded. Only the exceptional and the fortunate were allowed in. The majority were turned away. Most of them died in the Nazi concentration camps.

Yet for all the evil she found in racism and the Nazi movement, Dorothy could not accept war as a means of combating evil. "For eight years," she wrote, "we have been opposing the use of force—in the labor movement, in the class struggle, as well as in the struggles between countries." The Catholic Worker way, she said again and again, was the way of the cross, the only path to the resurrection. "War is the continuing passion of Christ," she wrote, "and Christ did not come down from the Cross to defend Himself."

Following the Japanese attack on Pearl Harbor and the U.S. declaration of war, *The Catholic Worker* published a banner headline which indicated that Dorothy's pacifist commitment was unshaken:

WE CONTINUE OUR CHRISTIAN PACIFIST STAND

"We will print the words of Christ who is with us always," Dorothy wrote in an editorial, "even to the end of the world. 'Love your enemies, do good to those who hate you, and pray for those who persecute and calumniate you, so that you may be children of your Father in Heaven, who makes His sun to rise on the good and the evil, and sends rain on the just and the unjust.' ... We are still pacifists. Our manifesto is the Sermon on the Mount, which means that we will try to be peacemakers. Speaking for many of our conscientious objectors, we will not participate in armed warfare or in making munitions, or by buying government bonds to prosecute the war, or in urging others to these efforts."

Opposition to the war, she went on, had nothing to do with sympathy for America's opponents in the war. "We love our country. ... We have been the only country in the world where men and women of all nations have taken refuge from oppression." But the means of action the Catholic Worker movement supported were the works of mercy rather than the works of war. "I would urge our friends and associates to care for the sick and the wounded, to the growing of food for the hungry, to the continuance of all our works of mercy in our houses and on our farms."

Many in the Catholic Worker movement could not agree with Dorothy. They could see no other effective means than war to combat Hitler. Nor could they accept that her convictions on such an issue should be presented as *the* position of the entire movement, in which hundreds were active in houses of hospitality all over the country. Dorothy appealed to friends and co-workers for mutual charity and patience. Faced with the war, many of the Worker's young men found that it was a time for battle rather than patience. They felt obliged to leave their hospices to enter the armed forces, as indeed did many of the men who previously had been on line waiting their turn for a bowl of soup. Lines shrank as the army and war industry absorbed millions who had been out of work. Fifteen houses of hospitality closed in the months following the U.S. entry into the war. John Cogley, a member of the Chicago Catholic Worker community, who later became a noted journalist, wrote Dorothy to say that he considered the Catholic Worker movement dead. "Now there is a group of pacifists defending their positions by calling attention to their good works and another group of diehards like myself who leave gracelessly. Peace! Peace! And there is no peace!" In a letter to Dorothy, one member of the Worker community in Milwaukee wrote of the conflict within her household, mourning the passage of tranquility and order that had held them together in the past. "Damn war!" she wrote. "Damn pacifism and stands! . . . How I wish you weren't a heretic. And sometimes how I wish that I were one too."

Following the big subscription losses during the Spanish Civil War, the movement had gained new support. *The Catholic Worker* printed 75,000 copies every month. But the pacifist position that the paper took after Pearl Harbor brought in a new wave of cancellations. Some argued theology or politics. The gentler letters asked questions, such as what Dorothy would do if an armed maniac threatened her daughter. "How many times have I heard this," Dorothy responded. "Restrain him, of course, but not kill him. Confine him, if necessary. But perfect love casts out fear and love overcomes hatred. All this sounds trite, I know, but experience is not trite."

Despite attrition, lost subscriptions, and division among co-workers, Dorothy's view was shared by many, and it prevailed in large measure simply because she wouldn't budge. She continued to edit *The Catholic Worker*, and every issue reaffirmed her understanding of the Christian life. Many issues that appeared during the wa. included a simple design: St. Francis standing beside the wolf he had tamed, accompanied by the words, "Peace without victory." At the New York house, an Association of Catholic Conscientious Objectors was founded to encourage and assist young

Catholic men of draft age who held pacifist views; among the committee's projects was publication of a newspaper, *The Catholic Conscientious Objector.*

Most of the houses of hospitality managed to remain open, despite smaller staffs. Dorothy traveled from house to house and spoke in public wherever there was a willingness to hear her. Surprisingly many invitations were offered.

The young men who identified with the Catholic Worker movement during the war generally spent much of the war years either in prison, or, more commonly, in rural work camps. Some others did unarmed military service as medics.

The Catholic Worker's pacifist witness seemed traitorous to the ultra-patriotic, embarrassing to many bishops, and suspiciously Protestant to some of the guardians of the customary. When *The Catholic Worker* urged young men not to register for the draft, Dorothy was summoned to the chancery office of the New York Archdiocese where a representative of Cardinal Spellman told her she had gone too far. On reflection, she agreed. "I realized that one should not tell another what to do in such circumstances. We had to follow our own consciences."

Even in correcting herself, as she did in the paper's next issue, Dorothy's cry against war, and her protest of Church complicity in it, was never muted. Wartime, she insisted, does not exempt us from the commandment to love our enemies and do good to those who curse us. "Our rule of life," she said repeatedly, "is the works of mercy."

A Lonely Single Parent

At the center of the Catholic Worker movement, with its many houses of hospitality and farms, its controversies and protest actions, stood Dorothy Day. By the mid-1930s she was already well known. In 1939, abandoning the fictional veneer she had used in her earlier book, she wrote a new autobiography, *From Union Square to Rome*, which one reviewer noted would have "created a sensation if it had been written in the form of a novel." At least one article by her appeared in every issue of *The Catholic Worker* and she was often writing for other publications. She was a "well known radical writer," it was said in *The Washington Star*, someone not only of interest to Catholics.

When not at the typewriter, she was often on the road, traveling among the scattered Catholic Worker communities and speaking at churches, colleges and union halls. Talking informally, always without notes, always with a cigarette, she impressed her many listeners with her convictions that the world would be remarkably improved if Christians were willing to search for the face of Christ in others, especially the poor and the condemned. "Those who cannot see Christ in the poor," she often said, "are atheists indeed." She was a Christian missionary, not to heathens but rather to fellow Christians, hoping to convert them to a faith they thought was theirs already. Her audiences found in her an example of what could be done by ordinary people, and by women, in a Church ruled by ordained men who rarely consulted the non-ordained and still less sought the advice or partnership of women.

Though her vocation involved daily engagement in the domain of human failure, still Dorothy experienced a kind of success. She was taken seriously by the hierarchy and even received encouragement and financial support from a few bishops. Through her and the movement she was leading, a great many people were finding a whole new direction and meaning in life. She was the focal point of much attention, much of which was admiring. Yet for all the conversions and new communities that had been inspired by her, and all the food and caring that had poured out of these communities, Dorothy still suffered her "long loneliness." She felt herself deeply alone and a failure in her most intimate relationships.

The demands of the Catholic Worker on Dorothy were such that the time she had for her daughter was greatly reduced once the movement began to be more than a newspaper. Apart from weekends and holidays, Tamar lived much of her childhood in a Catholic residential boarding school on Staten Island. Even when Tamar was home, Dorothy was often absorbed in meeting the needs of others. "There were plenty," Dorothy noted, "who laid claim to my sympathy and loving care to the extent of forgetting that I had personal family obligations." Some of the Catholic Worker guests were jealous of Tamar's place in Dorothy's life. One of these actually took Tamar's clothing and destroyed her collection of bird nests, egg cocoons and other natural specimens she had carefully gathered. At the Catholic Worker farm in Easton, an adobe village Tamar was building was wrecked by a guest who resented the time Dorothy gave to her daughter. These were ordeals for Dorothy as much as for Tamar, an awful consequence of being a single parent with competing responsibilities.

In the summer of 1936, Dorothy wrote in her journal about Tamar's problems of the day. She had suffered a nosebleed, a headache and stomach pain. Dorothy was dismayed at "the little time I have with her, being constantly on the go, having to leave her in the care of others, sending her away to school so that she can lead a regular life and not be subject to the moods and vagaries of the crowd of us! This is probably the cruelest hardship of all. She is happy, she does not feel torn constantly as I do. And then the doubt arises, probably she too feels I am failing her. ... Never before have I had such a complete sense of failure, of utter misery."

Dorothy missed being married. "A woman does not feel whole without a man," she confessed in autobiographical writing more than twenty years after her separation from Forster, "and for a woman who has known the joys of marriage, yes, it was hard. It was years before I awakened without the longing for a face pressed against my breast, and arm about my shoulder. The sense of loss was there."

She was deeply hurt when a priest told her, in the early years of the Catholic Worker, that her views would be quite different if she were a family woman. "I was going through a difficult time," she recalled. "I was thirty-eight, wishing I were married and living the ordinary naturally happy life and had not come under the dynamic influence of Peter Maurin."

As she dwelled on the priest's criticism, she realized that his perception of her—indeed her own perception of herself—was quite incomplete. "I *am* a woman of family. I have had a husband and home life—I have a daughter and she presents problems for me right now."

These problems became quite urgent during the Second World War when Tamar took a lively interest in the bright, attractive young men who were still coming as volunteers to the Catholic Worker. At the age of fifteen she was impatient with school and eager to marry. Dorothy responded with a search for a school offering courses more in line with Tamar's interests. In the fall Tamar entered an agricultural boarding school in Canada which taught spinning, weaving and other domestic crafts.

When Tamar, now sixteen, returned to the Catholic Worker farm at Easton the next summer, she fell in love with one of the new volunteers, David Hennessy. The two decided that they wanted to marry, farm together, and raise a family. Strongly opposing such plans, Dorothy did all she could to keep Tamar and David apart, bringing Tamar to New York as often as possible. In the fall she entered Tamar in a craft school in Rhode Island founded by a friend of Dorothy's, Ade Bethune, the artist who had designed the Catholic Worker symbol (the black and white workers with Jesus before the cross) and whose lino-cuts appeared in every issue. Though Tamar was a shy and retiring person, she persisted in her intention to marry David and resisted her mother in what ways she could.

No doubt Dorothy recognized in her daughter's struggle for independence and a home of her own troubling reminders of her own early departure from home and of her inability to give Tamar the kind of family life and stability her daughter urgently wanted. But Dorothy often found that the men at the Catholic Worker were more interested in talking about farms than doing farming. She may have anticipated that Tamar was soon to experience many of the bitter disappointments with men that she had known. In any event, it was immensely difficult to let go of her own child and the person who had become dearest to her. "I was always having to be parted from her," Dorothy wrote. Again and again she had been forced to give up those she loved: mother, younger brother, husband, and now daughter. It seemed no matter how many times she had to submit to such separations, "I had to do it over again."

She tried to persuade Tamar to go slow, to acquire useful skills, and to experience a time of independence before undertaking marriage. "I remember one time we were walking together down Mott Street," Dorothy wrote in an essay on marriage. "Tamar was walking close to my arm, clinging to me as she often did, and I warned her that she must learn to be self-reliant, to depend on herself, to learn to stand alone. I probably hurt her by so saying. We are always hurting those we love."

Tamar matched her mother in stubbornness, and finally Dorothy was forced to give way. The wedding Mass was celebrated in New York in April 1944, soon after Tamar's eighteenth birthday. In the austere circumstances of the Catholic Worker, there was neither bathtub nor mirror for Tamar's use as she prepared for the wedding. "She bathed in a pail the night before," Dorothy remembered, "and never did she know how lovely she looked in her wedding dress."

The next spring, Dorothy held in her arms her first grandchild, Rebecca. Seven more were born in the following years.

Retreats

"With the beginnings of the Catholic Worker, my working day began at early Mass . . . and often ended at midnight." Apart from times of prayer, there was never really a time of peace. The Worker way of life centered on permanent and inescapable crisis, not only because it was turned toward injustice and violence in the neighborhood and in the larger world but because of daily collisions with human need and suffering within the house: fights on the line, injuries, sickness, mental breakdowns, drunkenness, clashing personalities, ideological combat, hysterical or despairing individuals, empty bank accounts, theft or destruction of property, fires, evictions, demands from the city for costly alteration of buildings, withdrawal of co-workers to other places, and the interventions of death. A day without at least one crisis was rare for any Catholic Worker house, and Dorothy was uniquely linked to them all. Through letters and visits, their needs and difficulties were brought to her. Sometimes reluctantly, other times at her own insistence, she was the final arbiter of conflict within the Catholic Worker movement.

When coupled with periods of intense loneliness and her responsibilities as a mother, there were times when the burden seemed unbearable. To survive and find fresh inspiration, Dorothy continuously sought to deepen her spiritual life, which in the early years of the Catholic Worker came to include daily Mass, daily use of the rosary, short periods of communal or private prayer in the morning, afternoon and evening, religious reading, confession at least once a week, and reliance on the advice of a spiritual director.

On one occasion in the Catholic Worker's first years, Dorothy went for retreat to a contemplative monastery on East 28th Street, not far uptown from the Catholic Worker. Her stay proved a dry, depressing experience. The nuns lived an "enclosed life"—voluntary confinement within walls and behind grills that reminded her of prison bars. It was a cloistered life centered on prayer, the thought of which impressed Dorothy, but once there she found the situation too rarefied. "It was a hard time. When I left, I felt as if I was suddenly able to breathe again." She returned to the turbulent Catholic Worker household much readier to appreciate its highly unrarefied atmosphere. She preferred reading the writings of contemplative saints to seeking out the isolated kinds of places in which they had lived. And yet she sensed incompleteness in her spiritual life.

In 1939, Father Pacifique Roy, a French Canadian priest, came to visit. His work at the time was in Baltimore. Probably he had hitchhiked to New York, as that was his usual way of traveling. He welcomed the opportunity for talking with strangers. Despite a basic shyness, he was so possessed by his faith that he could readily talk about the stories and sayings of Jesus, doing so in a way that seemed to animate rather than irritate his drivers. He did the same at the Catholic Worker house, holding everyone spellbound. Hours passed, people arrived and left, the phone rang, but Father Roy continued to talk with the eager community that had gathered around him. "He spoke with such enthusiasm, with such joy," Dorothy remembered, and it was always so with him. "It was like the story in the Gospels, when the two apostles were talking on the way to Emmaus, grieving and fearful and lamenting over the death of their leader. Suddenly a fellow traveler came along and began to explain the Scriptures, going so far as the town with them and even going to an inn to break bread with them. They knew Him in the breaking of bread. They had to say to each other, 'Was not our heart burning within us, while he spoke on the way?' "

In Father Roy, Dorothy had at last found a priest who understood the Gospels as she did, who heard in them a call to a way of life which was profoundly revolutionary, and who recognized in the Catholic Worker movement a faithful response to that call. Here was someone with a gift for inspiring a deeper, more passionate spiritual life. Though days were weighted down with appalling news — the war in Europe, Hitler's growing empire, the doors of the United States and many other countries locked against so many Jews pleading for refuge — somehow the Worker staff was preserved from despair, and hope was given back. The day-to-day work of a house of hospitality struggling with so many needs and its own limitations — this too was transformed. "We saw all things new," wrote Dorothy. "There was a freshness about everything as though we were in love, as indeed we were."

At the time it would have been entirely unremarkable to hear one's parish priest explain that all you needed to do to be saved was follow the "precepts of salvation": heaven awaited those who were practicing Catholics, baptized and confirmed, who attended Mass on Sundays and holy days of obligation, went to confession, received Communion at least once a year, observed the marriage laws, raised their children as Catholics, and gave financial support to the Church. The emphasis was institutional, less a way of holiness than of obedience and conformity.

For Father Roy, such teaching utterly missed the point. Every word, every thought and prayer, every action should be infused with God's love. We are saved by love, not by keeping in line. "Love is the measure by which we shall be judged," he said repeatedly, quoting St. John of the Cross. The saying became a byword to Dorothy.

"To give and not to take," Peter Maurin often said, "that is what makes man human." Love, Father Roy said, is what makes us want to give. Giving is the essence of religious life: giving time and attention, giving prayer, giving possessions and money, giving space in one's life and home, giving a welcome, giving forgiveness, giving love, even giving one's life. Don't save. Don't store up "treasure which moth and rust attack." Live by the rule of giving.

"Suppose," Father Roy said, "you want to go to California and it costs a hundred dollars. You have fifteen. It is not enough. So give it away. Give it to the poor. Then you suddenly have twenty-five, and that is not enough and so the only thing to do is to give it away too. Even seventy-five. That is not enough. Tell the Lord you need more. Throw it away recklessly. You will get it back a hundredfold. Maybe it will cover your spiritual needs, and not just your physical. But sow, sow! And as you sow, so shall you reap. He who sows sparingly, reaps sparingly."

And what if you never get the hundred? Then stay where you are. "The good Lord knows what you need. Maybe you should not go to California!" His voice rang out with delight.

Dorothy began to take part in "days of recollection" that Father Roy occasionally led in Baltimore. In 1940 she wrote a lengthy letter to all the Catholic Worker communities urging all who could come from each house to take part in a retreat with Father Roy. More than an invitation, her letter was an introduction to the spirituality she hoped would become rooted in all those associated with the Catholic Worker movement.

She recalled a saying of St. Catherine of Siena: "All the way to heaven is heaven, because Jesus said, 'I am the way.' " It was also true, therefore, that "all the way to hell is hell." Heaven and hell are not simply ultimate destinations on the other side of death. Each can touch us in any moment of life. When we turn our backs on the needs of others, we fail to recognize Jesus, and we are in hell at that moment, for hell is not to love. To glimpse Christ in another, to love and care for another, is already to be in heaven. Life lived in awareness of the presence of God is a foretaste of heaven. Those who carry that awareness with them in their daily lives are saints, which ought not to be such a rare thing, for the world is in desperate need of saints. "We are all called to be saints," Paul had written, not having in mind the rare exception but ordinary people. It was a text once used as a *Catholic Worker* headline, stretching across the top of page 1. (But Dorothy always resisted the use of the word "saint" as a way of drawing a barrier between those who live saintly lives and their neighbors, and she was especially irritated whenever she herself was called a saint, sensing that she was being promoted to a special category of irrelevancy. "Don't call me a saint," she said on more than one occasion. "I don't want to be dismissed so easily.")

In response to Dorothy's letter, representatives of thirty houses of hospitality came together at the Worker farm in Easton. Other retreats followed in succeeding years. These were the center points in a process in which Dorothy's need to deepen her own spiritual life came to involve nearly everyone who identified with the Catholic Worker movement, as the retreats not only affected those who took part but profoundly influenced the content of the newspaper and the climate of every household in the Catholic Worker movement.

Most of the retreats in the war years were led not by Father Roy but another priest whom he had recommended to Dorothy, Father John Hugo of Pittsburgh. Father Hugo cherished a quotation from G. K. Chesterton and often repeated it: "Christianity has not been tried and found wanting. It has been found difficult and left untried. Even watered down, Christianity is still hot enough to boil the modern world to rags."

A writer as well as a retreat leader, Father Hugo's essays were often featured in *The Catholic Worker* and the Worker also published his work in book form, including *The Gospel of Peace* and *Applied Christianity.*

In retreats and writing he emphasized Christ's command that we forgive others, not sparingly but "seventy times seven" times, never withholding forgiveness. He emphasized Christianity's most difficult teaching, the love of enemies. The Christian is called not to answer blow with blow, but rather to respond to violence with kindness. He stressed sacrifice. Don't use what you don't need. Practice "voluntary poverty." Have as little as possible. The coat hanging in your closet on a winter day belongs to someone who is freezing without it: give it away. Do without. Do it for the love of others, especially for the poor, for Christ has hidden himself among the hungry and thirsty, the naked and homeless, the sick and imprisoned. Try to live as much as possible at a higher level, the level of the "supernatural," the level of love and the spiritual life. Supernatural action, action free of all selfishness, was paradoxically the only kind of action that brought with it an eternal reward, an increase. "Natural" actions would bring only a natural reward and would be swallowed up by the grave. Those who seek and obtain rewards, Jesus had taught in the Sermon on the Mount, "have their reward already."

"This was what I was looking for in the way of an explanation of Christian life," Dorothy exulted during a retreat with Father Hugo. "I saw things as a whole for the first time with a delight, a joy, an excitement which is hard to describe. This is what I expected when I became a Catholic."

In response to Father Hugo's encouragement, in the fall of 1943 Dorothy took a period of leave from the Catholic Worker in the midst of the war in order to experience a prolonged private retreat. A community of sisters in rural Long Island offered her an empty schoolroom which had formerly been used for cooking classes. Amid stoves and sinks, Dorothy made herself at home. She joined the sisters for daily Mass, prayed privately in the convent chapel, and took long walks. She was close to Tamar's school and the two often had an afternoon cup of hot chocolate together. Once a week Dorothy went by train to visit her mother. Generally, she was alone, struggling in her aloneness to go further in spiritual growth than she felt was possible in brief retreats. Her main work was prayer, which at times came with "joy and delight." More often she found herself in a state of utter boredom, her prayer only an act of will. She had meant to keep this retreat for a full year, but in the end six months was all she could stand. It was clear that a solitary life was not for her. "Man is not meant to live alone," she wrote with conviction afterward. "To cook for one's self, to eat by one's self, to sew, wash, clean for one's self is a sterile joy. Community, whether of family, or convent, or boarding house, is absolutely necessary."

Father Hugo had been not only Dorothy's spiritual director but in a sense was the spiritual director of the Catholic Worker movement during those years. All through World War II, he had been able to lead retreats, to publish, and to in every way maintain his close ties with the Catholic Worker — remarkable considering how out of step he was with many Catholic bishops and theologians at the time. Only after the war did he come under real attack. His bishop ordered him to stop giving retreats and to cease publishing. He accepted the order, quoting to friends the text, "Unless the seed fall into the ground and die, it remains alone, but when it dies, it bears much fruit."

At the chancery office of the New York Archdiocese, Dorothy was advised of the silencing and told that she should not again publish Father Hugo' s work. It must have been an appalling experience for her, but she complied, perhaps comforted by the thought that what he and Father Roy had done for her and for the Catholic Worker movement could not be undone. "Love is a commandment," Dorothy recalled in summing up what she had learned from Father Hugo. "It is a choice, a preference. If we love God with our whole hearts, how much heart have we left? If we love with our whole mind and soul and strength, how much mind and soul and strength have we left? We must live this life now. Death changes nothing. If we do not learn to enjoy God now we never will. If we do not learn to praise Him and thank Him and rejoice in Him now, we never will."

Breathing in the Dead

The end of the war, though a relief, was not an event Dorothy could celebrate. Hitler was dead, but militarism had survived, and fascism was only in hiding. The war had brought into existence many weapons of mass destruction, including the atom bomb. In a pair of blinding flashes, Hiroshima and Nagasaki—cities of minor industrial importance, one of them the center of Catholicism in Japan—had been destroyed. No one knew how many thousand had died in the war. For Dorothy it seemed that the real victor in 1945 wasn't the Allies but war and death, and that now death was armed with weapons capable of causing human extinction.

As she read the first reports of Hiroshima's destruction on August 6, Dorothy learned that President Truman was "jubilant." She thought about his name: "True man." How strange a name. "We refer to Jesus Christ as true God and true Man," she wrote in the September *Catholic Worker*. "Truman is a true man of his time in that he was jubilant about destruction. He was not a son of God, brother of Christ, brother of the Japanese, jubilating as he did." She thought of the vaporized dead, so like the dead of the Nazi concentration camps, "men, women and babies, scattered to the four winds over the seven seas. Perhaps we will breathe their dust into our nostrils, feel them on our faces in the fog of New York, feel them in the rain on the hills of Easton."

The press was full of news about how the bomb had been made, by what scientists and universities, at what secret, remote places the massive work had been carried on. Even God was given some of the credit. Press photos showed the large chapel beside the plant at Oak Ridge, Tennessee, where the fissionable material for the bomb had been processed. It was reported that scientists had prayed just before the first nuclear weapon was tested at Alamogordo, New Mexico. The test was code-named Trinity.

"But God is not mocked," Dorothy reflected. "We are held in God's hands, all of us, and President Truman, too. God holds our life and our happiness, our sanity and our health. Our lives are in His hands. He is our creator." *The* true Man came not to destroy but to save. He said, "What you did to the least person, you did to me."

Death touched Dorothy's life not only in dust, fog and rain, but in the loss of her mother in October. For years they had been seeing a great deal of each other. In the last weeks of Grace Day's life, Dorothy was at her bedside every day. "Do not pray that I live longer," she asked Dorothy. "I have been through two world wars, the San Francisco earthquake and a Florida hurricane, and I have had enough!"

Religious faith had not been a meeting point for Dorothy with her mother or any member of the family, but as Grace Day neared death, she asked Dorothy, "What about a future life?" Dorothy said she could no more imagine life beyond the grave than a blind man could imagine colors, but she pointed to a bouquet of violets near the bed. Flowers are like a promise from God, she said, "and God keeps His promises." She pointed to the trees outside the window, maples that had recently been blazing with color but now were being stripped of their leaves, seemingly dead. These maple trees were another sign of a promise, said Dorothy. After a while Grace Day said, "I can only pray the Our Father and the Creed. Is that enough?" Yes, Dorothy assured her. "It was like being present at a birth," said Dorothy, "to sit by a dying person and see her intentness on what was happening to her. . . . One is absorbed in a struggle, a fearful, grim, physical struggle, to breathe, to swallow, to live."

Before Grace Day's death, all traces of bitterness and fear seemed gone from her. "She sat up in bed," Dorothy recalled, "and, sipping on a cup of tea, remarked how comforting it was. She had taken up the little bouquet of violets, her favorite flower, and holding it to her face, smiled with happiness." She died the same day, October 24.

In the late 1940s, Peter Maurin was also approaching death. At the end of her six-month retreat in 1944, Dorothy came to visit him at the strife-ridden farm at Easton. She was distressed to discover how much he had aged in her absence. His voice lacked its usual vitality. He spoke slowly and had difficulty remembering names.

He gave his last talk at Tamar's wedding the next spring. He used the occasion to speak out against raising pigs for profit, though Tamar and David had no intention of raising pigs. "We all laughed, " Dorothy recalled, "but we all had to listen too. After all, it would not have been a Catholic Worker wedding without a speech from Peter."

By the end of the year Peter could not even recite his Easy Essays, which were so familiar to the staff that they could sing them out antiphonally with him as if they were Psalms. He gave his last manuscript to Arthur Sheehan, a member of the staff who later wrote the first biography of Peter, saying he had done enough, now it was up to the younger people. Within a few months his memory was gone. "He could no longer 'think,' as he tried to tell us sadly," Dorothy wrote.

In 1946, on the advice of a doctor, he received the last rites, the sacrament the Church offers to those facing death. In his sturdiness, however, Peter lived on. In 1947 he wandered off for several days and couldn't be found. Afterward notes with his name and address were put in his pockets. When the new farm and retreat center was purchased that spring in Newburgh, New York, it became Peter's new home. His room was a former chicken coop with a concrete floor, chosen for Peter as it was one of the farm's warmer structures.

Occasionally Peter's memory returned and he could think and make his "points" again. While in a New York hospital for ten days in December 1948, he was able to discuss the recently initiated "worker priest" movement in France. He was excited that such openings were being made in the barrier between the Church and the working class. Priests working in factories among those who wouldn't dream of attending Mass! This was what he had meant in proposing a "worker-scholar synthesis." But his inability to find words soon returned. His mouth often hung open. Friends sensed in him a painful struggle to comprehend what was going on. He died quietly in his room May 15, 1949.

The funeral Mass in New York City two days later was loud and triumphant, crowded not only with friends, Dorothy felt, but with angels and saints. In death as in life, he was dressed in castoff clothing contributed to the Catholic Worker. His burial plot was also donated. The undertaker tried to sell Dorothy artificial grass with which to cover the "unsightly grave." She refused, recalling how Peter loved the earth and rejoiced in working it with his hands.

His death was reported in the Vatican newspaper, *L'Osservatore Romano*, the editor aware that perhaps it was a saint who had died. Even *Time* magazine noted the passage of a joyful Christian who had embraced poverty and the poor while trying to build up a society in which it was easier "for people to be good."

Ammon

Late in the year of Peter Maurin's death, a cross-country speaking trip brought Dorothy to Phoenix, Arizona. Ammon Hennacy welcomed her at the bus station. She had met him only once before, very briefly, in 1937. From 1941 onward Dorothy had occasionally published Ammon's writings, while Ammon became one of the most committed distributors of the paper, hawking it outside local Catholic churches after Sunday Mass. He never took part in Mass himself. It was only after their Phoenix meeting in 1949 that Ammon began to center his life in the Catholic Worker, though already he was one of the movement's more spectacular figures.

Ammon — born in 1893 in rural Ohio — was tall and lanky, with a jutting chin, eagle nose, piercing blue eyes, and hair that seemed intended for a lion's mane. Like Peter, he was a man of radical ideas who was immediately at home in street-corner debate. But Ammon's temperament was quite different. Peter had agreed with some of the anarchist writers, especially Kropotkin, but preferred to call himself a "personalist" — a less alarming way of describing his refusal to conform or to obey civil law when he found it in violation of God's law. Ammon, though in action as nonviolent as Gandhi, enjoyed using words that went off like hand grenades. He gladly identified himself as an anarchist, whom he defined as someone "who doesn't need a cop to make him behave." The way to change the world, he said, was not by casting an occasional vote but by living the way that you wanted others to live. Each person could cause a revolution, "the one-man revolution," by self-transformation. For this you didn't have to wait for election day and hope your side won.

Ammon had come to a personal, un-churched Christian faith while reading the Bible in prison during the First World War. He had been convicted of refusal to register for the draft and spent two years in a federal penitentiary. During a period of solitary confinement, he argued within himself the pros and cons of the Sermon on the Mount. "The opposite of the Sermon on the Mount," he realized, "was what the whole world had been practicing, in prison and out of prison; and hate piled on hate had brought on hate and revenge. It was plain that this system did not work." He decided to use the Sermon on the Mount as the basis for his own life. Freed from prison after the war, he began a career in professional social work, but gave it up rather than pay taxes when the next world war began. He wasn't willing to pay for others to do what he wouldn't do himself. In 1943 he began "life at hard labor," doing farm work for cash wages from which no taxes were removed. He found the low pay and twelve-hour days in the field a challenge. He had, Dorothy wrote, "tremendous strength and endurance." In one of his occasional columns for *The Catholic Worker* (a piece reminiscent of Dorothy's "poverty squad" reporting) Ammon gave an account of how he lived on ten dollars a month: whole wheat flour, 25 lbs, $1.25; shortening, 3 lbs, .68; cornmeal, 5 lbs, .46; margarine, 2 lbs, .38; raisins, 2 lbs, .23.

Ammon was the only *Catholic Worker* regular contributor who was not only outside the Church but didn't like Catholicism. He objected to the Church's hierarchical structure, its elaborate ceremonies, its silence if not complicity in social injustice, its acceptance if not promotion of war, its wealth, its stress on obedience, its apparent indifference to conscience. His animosity toward Catholicism, expressed with a fierce dogmatism that few Popes would dare copy, led some of the Worker staff to call him "Father Hennacy."

"I didn't believe in the Church," he admitted, "but I believed in Dorothy." And she was deeply impressed with him. After their 1949 meeting she described him in her column as someone who wasn't just talking and protesting and refusing to take part in war but who was "trying to change the conditions that bring about war." Without benefit of the sacraments, she added, he was "doing the things we Catholics should be doing."

During Easter 1950, Ammon paid his first visit to the Worker house in New York where he readily expressed his reservations about the hospitality aspect. The community shouldn't waste its time "feeding bums," he said. And yet he found it difficult to leave. In 1952 he returned for a stay that lasted eight years.

His attraction was not only to the ideas that Catholic Workers were trying to live out but to Dorothy personally. For years he was ardently in love with her. He left only when he was drawn to another member of the community. While the love lasted, he poured it out to Dorothy in frequent notes and letters, even while expressing (one senses with reluctance) his admiration for Dorothy's celibacy.

Dorothy's feelings about Ammon are obscure. She was in her fifties and was still afflicted with a loneliness that was made only more acute by the admiration so many had for her. It may well be that she was grateful that Ammon not only found her admirable but attractive. She carefully kept his letters (in the open files of the Catholic Worker where anyone could read them). But she didn't respond to Ammon with similar letters.

Her published writings about him are quite dry-eyed. Ammon had a tendency, she wrote, to fall in love with women and had told her he couldn't remember a time when he wasn't in love with someone, and yet "he often spoke of women scornfully, insisting that they held men back in their radical careers." More troubling to her was his tendency to make "hasty judgments of others and his inability to see himself as ever in the wrong." He was the sort of person, irksome in his self-sufficiency, who "knows how to work, how to eat, to fast, to sleep, to meet each and every problem of the day." He often seemed to canonize himself in what he said about himself. But when she saw what he did rather than what he said, she was deeply moved. "When an extra bed was needed, he gave up his own over and over"—to the very "bums" about whom he had been complaining only moments before.

She was grateful for the energy and enthusiasm Ammon brought to the Catholic Worker. He had Peter's devotion to finding people where they were rather than waiting for them to walk through the door. A large part of Ammon's day was given over to standing on the streets selling *The Catholic Worker.* In the course of each week he made his way from Wall Street, in lower Manhattan, to the Fordham University campus uptown in the Bronx. Over the years thousands came to recognize him, and hundreds— among them bankers and professors—were regular partners in friendly debate. Some became admirers and friends, including Steve Allen, the television humorist, who wrote the introduction to Ammon's self-published autobiography, *The Book of Ammon.* "Ammon," he wrote, "has *experienced*—not just read about—atheism, socialism, anarchism, pacifism, communism, anti-communism, violence, poverty, civil disobedience, Christianity, Protestantism, Catholicism, Mormonism, picket lines, freedom rides, imprisonment, hunger, manual labor, farming, vegetarianism, despair, faith, hope and love." This was far from a complete list, he added, but at least it indicated Ammon's "zest for bare, natural, principled life. . . . Even if Ammon were mistaken on every one of his fundamental beliefs and assumptions—which is true of no one—we could still learn something from him because of his love of the world."

Ammon's respect for Dorothy and her commitment to the Catholic Church was such that, to her joy and astonishment, he became a Catholic himself in November 1952. Fifteen years later, when his local bishop failed to intervene on behalf of two men awaiting execution, he withdrew. He had become a Catholic, he said in his final years, because of Dorothy. If she had been a Mormon and had edited *The Mormon Worker*, he would have become a Mormon.

Even so, he remained a part of the Catholic Worker movement for the rest of his life. If no longer a convert to Catholicism, he was a convert to the "bums." After leaving the New York house in 1961, he founded a new Worker center in Salt Lake City, Utah, where he remained until his death in 1970. It was named the Joe Hill House of Hospitality and St. Joseph Refuge. Joe Hill—the anarchist labor organizer and songwriter—had long been among Ammon's saints. Joe Hill's best known song, often heard on picket lines and in union halls during the Depression, was a parody of a religious hymn. Ammon loved its irreverent refrain:

Work and pray,
live on hay—
You'll get pie in the sky when you die.

Cold War

The U.S.-Soviet alliance against Hitler had culminated joyously when the victorious armies met at the Elbe River in central Germany on April 25, 1945. Without a common enemy, their relations began to deteriorate, beginning a process of world polarization and "Cold War." Early in 1946, while visiting the United States, Winston Churchill called for a post-war alliance against Soviet Communism, which had drawn an "iron curtain" across Europe. In 1947, the United States initiated a massive aid program to non-Communist Europe and, in 1946, presided over the formation of an alliance such as Churchill had imagined, the North Atlantic Treaty Organization. It was the traumatic year of the Berlin Airlift. The following year, Communists came to power in China.

But no post-war event shocked Americans so much as the successful explosion of an atom bomb by the Soviet Union in August 1949. Congressman Richard Nixon, a member of the House Committee on Un-American Activities, was among the first to blame the Soviet achievement on "Red spies" in the United States. In February 1950, Senator Joseph McCarthy told a Women's Republican Club in West Virginia that he had in his possession a list of Communists employed within the State Department. Though he refused to reveal any names, his speech was front-page news across America. The McCarthy era was underway, a long and nasty season of suspicion and fear.

J. Edgar Hoover, Director of the Federal Bureau of Investigation, initiated a nationwide spy hunt for those who, he charged, had "betrayed American secrets to the Kremlin." In the summer of 1950 Julius and Ethel Rosenberg, two Communists living in New York, were arrested and accused of passing on atom bomb secrets to the Soviet Union. Three years later, still protesting their innocence, the two died in the electric chair.

For years "the enemy within" was a major theme in American political life. The Communist Party was outlawed, its members regarded as agents of a foreign power. A Communist was defined as anyone whose political views in any way resembled those taken by the Communist Party. Those who advocated peace or disarmament, who protested racial segregation or criticized capitalism, were likely to be called, if not Communists, "pinkos" or "fellow travelers." Suspected Communists were purged from leadership roles in labor unions. Teachers and civil servants were required to sign "loyalty oaths." The mere suspicion of Communist sympathies or a Communist past cost many their livelihood. Nor was the Communist Party the only target. The Attorney General drew up a list of "Communist-front" organizations. "The only good Red is a dead Red," ran a popular slogan of the American 1950s.

The clergy were often as fervent as politicians and editorial writers in denouncing Communism, but perhaps no major Christian church was so renowned for its anti-Communism as the Catholic Church. Pope Pius XII, though he was among those who appealed to President Eisenhower to spare the Rosenbergs' lives, declared that any Catholic collaborating with Communists was excommunicated.

Many hands reached out to welcome and reward those who repented of their radical past, if the repentance was proved by a readiness to speak out against Communism and to "name names" — to testify against those who had been, still were or even seemed to be Communists.

Dorothy was often accused of being a Communist. Even some of those who knew it wasn't true were disturbed by her continuing friendships with such prominent Communists as Mike Gold and Elizabeth Gurley Flynn. Far from disowning them, Dorothy was among the few who spoke up for Flynn and ten other leading Communists when they were arrested and charged with "conspiring to advocate the overthrow of the United States government by force and violence."

As only lawyers tended to realize, none of those arrested were accused of violence or even the advocacy of violence. It was entirely a conspiracy indictment. They were accused of "conspiring to advocate" — being part of a movement with "a lot of cloak but no dagger," as one Communist commented.

When Dorothy protested that the jailed Communists should be allowed freedom on bail while they prepared their defense, the *Worker* received a wave of angry letters and subscription cancellations. Far from backing off, Dorothy replied with a column emphasizing her debt to Communists:

"I can say with warmth that I loved the Communists I worked with and learned much from them. They helped me to find God in His poor, in His abandoned ones, as I had not found Him in the Christian churches. . . . My radical associates were the ones who were in the forefront of the struggle for a better social order where there would not be so many poor." She pointed out that Christianity has points in common with Communism. It was a Christian ideal that Marxists had borrowed in advocating, "From each according to his ability, to each according to his need." Dorothy shared Marx's hope that the state would eventually wither away. She disagreed with Communists about violence, but in this, she added, she disagreed with Republicans and Democrats as well, and with many Christians, so many of whom endorsed violence and war when other political methods failed: "If only we who follow Christ had the zeal for the exploited workers and the poor that one regularly finds among Communists!"

An Order To Change

The Catholic Worker's Name

The identification of Communists with unions, protests and calls for social justice was so automatic in the post-war years that when a small union of gravediggers went out on strike against the Archdiocese of New York in 1949, Cardinal Spellman told the press that the men were Communist inspired. He refused to meet them and ordered seminarians to dig the graves until the strike was crushed. The strikers responded with an oath that their only motive was their economic problems and that Communism had nothing to do with it.

Dorothy had always emphasized her respect for the bishops, and for Cardinal Spellman personally, but she quickly came to the side of the grave-diggers, expressing her regret for the cardinal's "show of force" in making seminarians into strike-breakers. She took part in the union's meager picket line in front of the cardinal's palatial office behind St. Patrick's Cathedral on Madison Avenue and wrote of them in her column as "victims of that most awful of all wars, the war between clergy and laity." In a letter to the cardinal, she begged him to realize that the strikers were not only seeking better wages and working conditions but "their dignity as men." Dorothy begged him, as "a prince of the Church, and a great man in the eyes of the world," to meet personally with the strikers and open himself to their appeal. "They want to talk to you, and, oh, I do beg you so with all my heart to go to them." There was no response either to Dorothy or to the men. The strike was defeated within a month.

Her public criticism of the cardinal and participation in what was surely the first picket line of lay Catholics in front of any bishop's chancery, and her refusal to condemn Communists, were the kinds of events sure to be long remembered by Cardinal Spellman, who was outspoken in his views on the "Red menace" and a strict believer in obedience and conformity within the Church. In March 1951, Dorothy received a request from a member of his staff, Msgr. Edward Gaffney, to come to the chancery office.

"He told me we would have to cease publication or change our name," Dorothy recalled.

Msgr. Gaffney may well have expected Dorothy's prompt compliance. "We recognize and accept the authority of the Church as we do that of Christ himself," she had written at the time of the gravediggers' strike. She had often said she would put obedience to her bishop above continuation of her newspaper if she had to make the choice.

But she told Msgr. Gaffney that she needed to give this more thought and, after all, it wasn't only for her to decide. She needed to consult with those who shared in editorial responsibility for *The Catholic Worker.*

A few days later she responded by letter, reaffirming her "love and respectful obedience to the Church, and our gratitude to this Archdiocese, which has so often and so generously defended us from the many who attack us." She did not, however, wish to take advantage of such kindness "nor count on the official protection which the name Catholic brings us." Therefore she was *personally* willing to change the paper's name rather than to cease publication. However, the *others* involved in editing the paper were not willing to make such a change. "All feel that *The Catholic Worker* has been in existence for eighteen years . . . under that name, and that this is no time to change it." She pointed out that the Catholic War Veterans, an independent lay movement, was under no pressure to change its name. Should not the Catholic War Veterans and the Catholic Worker be equally free to express their points of view without being held as representing the official views of the Archdiocese? She appealed for dialogue instead of suppression. "We are all ready to receive respectfully and give practical heed and application to all scientific, scholarly criticism and correction of mistakes . . . and to all theological or spiritual censures of theological or spiritual errors." But, she went on, in effect saying no to the order, "we cannot simply cease the publication of a review which has been built up, with its worldwide circulation of 63,000. . . . This would be a grave scandal to our readers and would put into the hands of our enemies, the enemies of the Church, a formidable weapon." She regretted that she had not herself given more time to her editorial responsibility and promised to take a firmer hand. "Whether or not I am at fault," she went on, "I and my associates have spent years" trying to publish a journal which encourages its readers to build up "a new society within the shell of the old . . . [a] cooperative order as opposed to the corporate state." She pointed out that Catholics were not by definition capitalists or committed to capitalism and that the Vatican's own newspaper, *L'Osservatore Romano*, had criticized not only the Soviet but the American economic systems. Both were deeply flawed. And *The Catholic Worker* was flawed too. She promised to "try to be less dogmatic, more persuasive, less irritating, more winning."

The order from the Archdiocese was dropped. A change of heart in the chancery office? A tactical withdrawal? Perhaps a little of both.

As for the content of *The Catholic Worker* following Dorothy's letter, one finds no change, though Dorothy took a more active part in reading submissions.

Her own position was significantly strengthened in January 1952 when her autobiography, *The Long Loneliness*, was published by Harper & Row. The book was widely and favorably reviewed, sold well, and has been almost continually in print ever since. The same year Dwight Macdonald wrote an admiring two-part essay about Dorothy for *The New Yorker*.

It would have been understandable if Dorothy had withdrawn from any public activities on behalf of Communists and had stopped writing about them in the paper, in order to be "less irritating, more winning," at least to the cardinal. But she was deeply and publicly troubled about the arrest of the Rosenbergs and even appealed to Cardinal Spellman to oppose their execution.

One of her most beautiful essays for *The Catholic Worker* was her "Meditation on the Death of the Rosenbergs" published in the issue following their execution June 19, 1953. That evening she bathed one of her grandchildren, Nickie, while praying for the condemned couple: "God, let them be strong, take away all fear from them, let them be spared this suffering, at least this suffering of fear and trembling." She recalled Dostoyevsky, who had been sentenced to death and then was spared at the last moment, and she continued to hope against hope that there might still be a reprieve. She thought of Albert Einstein and Harold Urey, who had declared their belief in the innocence of the Rosenbergs. But what if they were guilty, she wondered, as President Eisenhower and Cardinal Spellman believe? "Even so, what should be the attitude of the Christian but one of love and great yearning for salvation?"

Soon after Nickie's bath was over, the jazz music on the radio was interrupted to give the bulletin reporting the Rosenbergs' deaths. In the morning, Dorothy carefully read the detailed account in *The New York Times*. "A rabbi who had attended them to the last said that they had been his parishioners for two years. He followed them to the execution chamber reading from the psalms, the 23rd, the 15th, the 31st. Those same psalms Cardinal Spellman reads every week as he reads his breviary. . . ."

"How mixed up religion can become," she wrote. How little our activities are shaped by the holy words we know by heart. Christian prelates "sprinkle holy water on scrap metal to be used for obliteration bombing, and name bombers for the Holy Innocents or for Our Lady of Mercy [and] bless a man about to press a button which releases death on fifty thousand human beings. . . ."

She was grateful to learn that the Rosenbergs had gone to their deaths firmly and quietly, expressing their love for their children and professing their innocence. "At the last Ethel turned to one of the two police matrons who accompanied her and, clasping her by the hand, pulled her toward her and kissed her warmly. Her last gesture was one of love."

Laughter in the Park

In the spring of 1955, the New York press reported that a statewide civil defense drill was scheduled for June 15. The news came with a warning: anyone refusing to take shelter (going into basements or subways, crouching in hallways or under desks in schoolrooms) risked up to one year in prison and a $500 fine. The message underlying the drill was that nuclear war was a real possibility but that, if the right steps were taken, it was survivable. A national shelter industry sprang to life despite warnings from those familiar with the effects of nuclear explosions that all the buyer got for his money was a larger-than-average coffin, while those who did survive their underground confinement would find a radioactive world far better suited to insect than human life. One peace group, the Fellowship of Reconciliation, responded by launching a "Shelters for the Shelterless" campaign, as a result of which thousands of small houses were built for homeless people in India. The same group printed a sign which families brave enough to risk the accusation of Communism put on their front doors:

THIS HOUSE HAS NO FALLOUT SHELTER

Peace is our only protection.

News of the forthcoming shelter drill caught Ammon Hennacy's eye. He proposed to those at the Catholic Worker house and to other pacifists in New York that this was a foolish and malicious law well worth breaking.

On June 15, Dorothy, Ammon and a handful of others met in the park in front of City Hall in lower Manhattan. When the air raid sirens began to wail, cars and buses pulled to the curb and New Yorkers drained into cellars and subway stations. Within minutes New York, playing war rather than business, seemed silent and abandoned. At City Hall Park, Dorothy and the other pacifists (not only from the Worker but from War Resisters League and the Fellowship of Reconciliation) stayed where they were, looking more like picnickers than protesters. While television cameras filmed their quiet witness, police escorted the lawbreakers into vans and drove them off.

To most Americans, it must have seemed a particularly ridiculous gesture: Surely the drill was only for everyone's safety? And the law is the law. And the Russians are not only the ruthless atheists they used to be, people with no principles and no respect for human life, but they are armed with nuclear weapons. What was one to make of the Catholic Worker leaflet, so completely at odds with the Cold War religious declarations of the 1950s: "In the name of Jesus, who is God, who is Love, we will not obey this order to pretend, to evacuate, to hide. . . . We will not be drilled into fear. . . . We do not have faith in God if we depend upon the Atom Bomb."

In a more personal statement, Dorothy emphasized that her refusal to take shelter was not only a protest against war and preparations for war, but "an act of penance" undertaken by an American whose country "had been the first to drop the atom bomb and to make the hydrogen bomb."

At 11 P.M. the ten appeared in night court. One of them, the actress Judith Malina, saw no reason to address the judge as "Your Honor" and didn't. He responded by asking if she had ever been in a mental institution. "No," she replied, "have you?" Those in the courtroom laughed, but not the judge, who ordered Judith to be taken for observation at the Bellevue psychiatric ward. For the others he set $1,500 bail, a sum associated with serious crimes. ("Well, it was a serious crime," said one member of the Catholic Worker community. "We were defying the White House. We were defying the Pentagon. We were defying the governor. We were defying the national mood. We were defying the habit of war. We were refusing to get ready for war.")

Dorothy and the others refused to provide bail, but after twenty-four hours were sent home without sentence or fine by a friendlier judge. "All we got was a slap on the wrist," one of them said. But even a day had given Dorothy time to kneel on the floor of her cell—"a bare, stark cell that would outdo the Carmelite in austerity"—and "thank God for the opportunity to be there, to be so stripped of all that the earth holds dear, to share in some way the life of prisoners, guilty and innocent, all over the world."

A year later, the drill was repeated, as was the protest in City Hall Park. The demonstrators were ordered to pay a fine or serve five days in jail. (One of those who opted for the fine was David Caplan, a physicist, who tried to convince the judge that civil defense preparations in a city like New York were dishonest: one would need to be far deeper—not in a subway tunnel just under the street—to have any hope of survival.)

Dorothy chose jail. The poor couldn't pay fines, she said, which was one of the reasons the jails were full of the poor. Also, Jesus had said, "I was a prisoner and you came to be with me."

Again in 1957, she was jailed. By then Dorothy's disobedience seemed a kind of urban ritual, like painting a green stripe down Fifth Avenue on St. Patrick's Day. The press, in greater numbers than ever, came to watch the pacifists get loaded into paddy wagons, this time on Chrystie Street, in the Catholic Worker's own neighborhood. The judge, a Catholic, advised

Dorothy to read the Bible and said that those who disobeyed the civil defense laws were a "heartless bunch of individuals who breathe contempt." He imposed a thirty-day sentence.

Putting Dorothy Day in jail was something like throwing Br'er Rabbit into the briar patch. "It is good to be here, Lord," Dorothy wrote from her cell in the Women's House of Detention in Greenwich Village, not far from the bar where she used to drink with Eugene O'Neill. "We were, frankly, hoping for jail," she admitted. Being in jail, one could come closer to real poverty. "Then we would not be running a house of hospitality, we would not be dispensing food and clothing, we would not be ministering to the destitute, but we would be truly one of them."

It was, in fact, a shocking, grinding experience — "crushing, numbing and painful at the same time." It wasn't just the abrasive, sack-like clothing, the constant assault of the mind by noise, the small and crowded cells, or the sexual harassment being suffered by so many of the younger inmates. What was most difficult was the deep sadness and despair that filled the prison. So many prisoners could look toward the future only with dread. Dorothy left prison, she wrote in *The Catholic Worker*, in a state of mental, physical and even spiritual exhaustion, yet grateful for the experience and ready to face the same consequences next summer. "It is a gesture, perhaps, but a necessary one. Silence means consent, and we cannot consent to the militarization of our country without protest. Since we believe that air raid drills are part of a calculated plan to inspire fear of the enemy, instead of the love which Jesus Christ told us we should feel, we must protest these drills. It is an opportunity to show we mean what we write when we repeat over and over that we are put here on this earth to love God and our neighbor."

The longer jail term made Dorothy think again of the need for a completely different response from society to those accused or convicted of crimes. She had seen the ways in which prisons damage those who live or work in them, making many inmates only more angry and dangerous than they were before, while reducing others to an awful, passive brokenness. Would not more be accomplished in small, homelike settings in which prisoners were recognized as persons of value and promise? In prison, staff was mainly hired to guard inmates, not "to love them." She envisioned rural centers at which the inmates raised much of their own food, baked their own bread, milked cows, tended chickens, engaged in creative activity and shared responsibility for the institution so that it wasn't a static environment but was, "in its own way, a community." Prison as it exists, she found, was the very opposite of community. The prisoner is simply an object which can be stripped and searched in the crudest possible ways — in the case of women prisoners, "even to the tearing of tissues so that bleeding results."

Why, she asked, were Christians so blind to Christ's presence in these people? "Christ is with us today, not only in the Blessed Sacrament and where two or three are gathered together in His Name, but also in the poor. And who could be poorer and more destitute in body and soul than these companions of ours in prison?"

In 1958, Dorothy and Ammon, with seven others, again stayed above ground as an imaginary nuclear explosion occurred in New York. The judge suspended sentence. In 1959 there were fourteen; five of them, including Dorothy and Ammon, served five-day jail terms. The judge was a kindly man, but found that they were failing to render to Caesar the things that are Caesar's, which prompted Ammon to reply, "Caesar has been getting too much around here and someone has to stand up for God."

One of the early hints that Americans were going to be very different in the 1960s than they had been in the 1950s was the crowd that gathered with Dorothy in front of City Hall on May 3, 1960. When the air raid sirens howled, five hundred stood in the park and another five hundred on the sidewalks across the street. Laughter greeted police orders to take shelter. In the arrests that followed, it seemed obvious that they were under orders not to arrest Dorothy Day, but twenty-five others were punished with five-day sentences. The demonstrators, however, were no longer a subject for editorial ridicule. The conservative *New York World Telegram* said that the war drills were "an exercise in futility." Civil defense would work, the paper added, only if "the enemy's plan is to drop marshmallow puffs." An article in *The New York Post* was headlined, "Laughter in the Park."

The following spring at least two thousand gathered in cheerful disobedience at City Hall Park. The police arrested a symbolic forty. Once again, Dorothy and Ammon were bypassed, to their disappointment. Nor was protest confined to the neighborhood of the mayor's office. All over New York, the sirens seemed to call people onto the streets rather than underneath. It proved too much for the politicians. New York had no more civil defense drills.

Revolutionary Sitting

While the New York press gathered to watch Dorothy and others sitting quietly on park benches during air raid drills, no journalist had been present to witness the act of illegal sitting on a bus in Montgomery, Alabama. On December 1, 1955, Mrs. Rosa Parks, a seamstress and a devout Christian much respected in Montgomery's black community, refused to give up her seat to a white man. Tired from her day of work, she simply stayed where she was. The driver summoned a policeman who seemed embarrassed at the job which had come to him. "Why didn't you stand up?" he asked Mrs. Parks. "I don't think I should have to," she replied. "Why do you push us around?" "I don't know," said the policeman, "but the law's the law, and you are under arrest." He drove Mrs. Parks to the jail, where she was then locked up. "I don't recall being extremely frightened," she said afterward, "but I felt very much annoyed and inconvenienced because I had hoped to go home and get my dinner, and do whatever else I had to do for the evening. But now here I was sitting in jail and couldn't get home."

Her quiet act of self-respect awakened a new will among Montgomery blacks to resist segregation. Some had been waiting for just such a moment, among them a young pastor who had only recently come to Montgomery, Dr. Martin Luther King, Jr. He was a Georgian, and among the rare Christians in America who had a special interest in Gandhi. Four days after Mrs. Parks' arrest, Dr. King was elected president of a new organization, the Montgomery Improvement Association, and a black boycott of the city buses began. Black people would rather walk than return to segregated buses, Dr. King announced. Mrs. Parks had been "anchored to that seat," he said, "by the accumulated indignities of days gone by and the boundless aspirations of generations yet unborn."

Almost unnoticed in the boycott's first days, "an experiment in the power of unarmed truth" had begun in Alabama which did much to bring into existence a new, revitalized national civil rights movement. In just over a year, despite much violence against blacks in Montgomery and the bombing of Dr. King's home, the city buses were peacefully integrated.

Dorothy was elated. At last America was taking seriously a way of struggle which sought conversion rather than defeat of opponents, a nonviolent way to overcome injustice. Nonviolence was suddenly a word in American usage. What she had long seen in the Gospels was being practiced by increasing numbers of ordinary people, some of whom were murdered and many beaten and imprisoned. The kind of sacrifice pacifists were making in New York was very little in comparison. In New York's jail cells, they were more comfortable, better fed, and even safer than many of America's poor.

Dorothy's special interest in community had long made her aware of Koinonia, a Christian agricultural community at Americus, in rural Georgia, where blacks and whites had been quietly living together since 1942. Koinonia (the Greek word for community) had been founded by Clarence and Florence Jordan, local people well aware of the anger many felt toward any who ignored racial segregation. Clarence Jordan, a white Baptist pastor, was a biblical scholar. In his spare time he translated the ancient Greek New Testament into the language of rural Georgia — *The Cotton Patch Translation*, as he called it. He was able to say hard things in a comic way in his sermons and conversations. He liked to tell the story of a minister who boasted that his congregation was so committed to the church that they had raised ten thousand dollars to put a gilded cross on top of the steeple. "You got cheated!" Clarence told him. "Times were when Christians could get them for free."

The bus boycott in Montgomery, and the Supreme Court decision overturning segregation in education, angered and threatened those committed to racial separation. Tensions rose in Americus as they did in many towns and cities, and in the neighborhood some began to think it would be a good thing if there was no more Koinonia.

Early in 1956, soon after the house of the King family was bombed in Montgomery, Koinonia began receiving threatening phone calls. Local people who had been buying eggs and other produce from the community farm canceled their orders. Sales started dropping at their roadside farm stand. Store owners in Americus refused to sell to Koinonia. Just after the U. S. Supreme Court decided that segregation of city buses was unconstitutional, some shots were fired at the community farm stand, and a month later — July 1956 — the stand was demolished by a dynamite blast. In November, a refrigerated meat case was destroyed by gunfire. The day after Christmas, the community fuel pump was shot to ruins. In January one of the Koinonia houses was hit by machine-gun fire. In February other houses were targets, and Ku Klux Klan members burned crosses on community land.

The same month Dorothy decided to spend some days with the community, wanting to meet those she knew only by name, and to keep Lent by sharing in their trials and hopes. She arrived in Americus after a day and night of bus travel from New York and immediately got a taste of local anger. Driving with Florence Jordan to towns in the area, she saw that no one was willing to sell seed to Koinonia. On the streets, people followed them shouting "nigger lovers" and "dirty communist whores."

Refusing the advice of her hosts, Dorothy insisted on taking a turn at the sentry post the community had set up by a large oak tree at the entrance to Koinonia. Easter Eve, her thoughts centered on Jesus' arrest and suffering, she waited in a station wagon—simply sitting, like Mrs. Parks on her bus. She noticed an approaching car had reduced its speed. She ducked just as the car was hit by rifle fire. One bullet struck the steering column in front of her face.

Dorothy was deeply shaken, but alive and without injury. She said little of the event in her writing, though one senses her gratitude to have finally been present with those who were daily risking their lives in following the way of the Cross. For herself, she said, she had "not yet resisted unto blood."

Koinonia survived its siege, and today lives on friendly terms with its neighbors.

Concordances, Not Differences

On October 9, 1958, the College of Cardinals elected a successor to Pope Pius XII: Angelo Roncalli, the seventy-six-year-old Archbishop of Venice. Journalists reporting the event assumed that the Catholic Church would experience a few quiet years under the gentle care of an elderly traditionalist.

The cardinals might as well have elected Dorothy Day to occupy the throne of Peter. This large, homely Italian, while most orthodox and pious, proved to be a revolutionary. The duty of the Pope, Roncalli explained, was not only to guard the treasure of faith but to devote himself, "with joy and without fear, to the work of giving this ancient and eternal doctrine a relevancy corresponding to the conditions of our era."

He chose the name John (unused by bishops of Rome since the fourteenth century) and in his first message after election quoted from the Gospel of John: "My children, love one another. Love one another because this is the greatest commandment of the Lord."

The new Pope had a disarming, cheerful manner that contrasted sharply with the austere personality of Pius XII. John communicated both to believer and unbeliever a special warmth. Church leaders so often seemed remote, legalistic and condemning, while John was a man of accessibility, expectancy and welcome. In one area in particular, the contrast was stunning. Pius XII had excommunicated Catholics who cooperated with Communists, while John appealed to Catholics not to allow any political and religious divisions—even between Marxism and Christianity—to impede cooperation in the service of peace and the common good. Granting a private audience to the nephew of the Soviet premier, Nikita Khrushchev, Pope John gave an unprecedented example of Christian-Marxist encounter. Doors in Rome that had long been double-locked were suddenly opening.

He had been Pope barely three months when he surprised the world, and astonished the cardinals, by announcing his intention to convene a council, only the second such event in four hundred years. It had been nearly a century since the First Vatican Council, an event cut short by the military occupation of Rome and the fall of the Papal States. That council's only memorable accomplishment had been its proclamation that, in matters of faith and morals, the Roman Pontiff could speak with infallibility. It was a dogma that had occasioned a schism, widening the distance between Catholics and other Christians, and a century later it remained a point of bitter theological controversy even within Catholicism.

This new council, said John, would declare no dogmas, issue no condemnations or excommunications, and do nothing to inflame hostility or to sanction enmity. It would be a "pastoral" council helping to restore "the simple and pure lines that the face of the Church of Jesus had at its birth."

"We must seek concordances, not differences," said the Pope, words Dorothy often repeated in the years that followed. It was advice summarizing her commitment of long standing to seek areas of agreement and cooperation with those whom Catholics had so often regarded as enemies to be met only in combat.

During the same month that Pope John announced his plan for a council — January 1959 — a revolution led by a young, radical lawyer, Fidel Castro, achieved victory in the small Catholic country of Cuba, just ninety miles from Florida. While many Americans were alarmed by the event, and various U.S. government agencies began to explore means to kill Castro and overthrow the Cuban revolution, Dorothy greeted the new regime in Cuba with hope. Here was a situation in which we should be seeking, she said, "concordances, not differences."

On April 17, 1961, twelve hundred anti-Castro Cuban exiles landed at the Bay of Pigs on the southwestern coast of Cuba. They had been trained and supplied by the U.S. Central Intelligence Agency, which believed the landing would spark a country-wide counter-revolution. In fact the invasion only unified the Cuban people. Most of the invaders were captured alive — more than a thousand — and were later returned to the United States in exchange for food and medicine.

One of the few *Catholic Worker* readers in Cuba, Mario Gonzalez, wrote to Dorothy appealing for help. He wondered if it would not be possible for some Catholic bishops from the United States to come to Cuba on "a journey of reconciliation" to demonstrate that "the Church is really interested in uniting all Christians under one banner of humility and love." Perhaps even "the new, healthy Pope" would come and make an appeal from Cuba, asking Americans "to give up hatred." The bishops and cardinals in Cuba, he added, had been close to the former corrupt government. They had enjoyed much power and wealth and needed a "lesson in humility" that would inspire them to stop living like royalty and to turn their estates into houses of hospitality, schools and hospitals.

Rather than urge any bishop to make such a journey, Dorothy decided to go herself. For eighty dollars she bought a tourist class ticket for a round-trip voyage from Jersey City to Havana (one of the last commercial tickets to Cuba sold in the United States in that decade, as it turned out). After weeks of daily tutoring in Spanish at the Berlitz School in New York, Dorothy sailed aboard the *Guadalupe*, a Spanish ship on which Mass was celebrated daily.

Arriving in Havana on September 8, 1962 after three days at sea, Dorothy's first errand was to deliver to the National Hospital several cartons of medical supplies. She checked into a small hotel and after a few days was able to obtain a press card. It was almost immediately cancelled — all credentials issued to American journalists were withdrawn by the government in light of the rapidly deteriorating relations between the two countries. But before the courier brought the cancellation order to Dorothy's hotel, she had checked out. "I was sitting on my suitcase in a long line in the bus station, in a mob of soldiers, *campesinos*, and their wives and children." At about four in the morning, Dorothy began the eighteen-hour passage to Oriente Province, the eastern tip of Cuba, on the first of many overcrowded buses that carried her little by little around the island. Her plan was to have an unguided and unmonitored look at ordinary Cubans and their country. She was not interested in political reporting but in offering her readers what Thomas Merton had called "the human dimension."

In her diary, published over several months in *The Catholic Worker*, Dorothy described her encounters with people ignored by the mass media. She told of families living in dirt-floor houses in areas still without electricity where old and young gathered around oil lamps at night to learn to read. She took note of what she found on the shelves in village shops: tins of evaporated milk, pencils and paper, and books. Everywhere she noticed schools and clinics being opened. Despite the hardship and shortages, it seemed to her that the people were animated by hope. In earlier times the land had either belonged to U.S. companies or to the few wealthy Cuban families — now it was theirs. Poverty remained, but the old serfdom was finished. The alphabet and books were finding their way into every family.

Writing for Americans whose press was emphasizing the exodus of many priests from Cuba, and the tensions between the Church and the Communist government, Dorothy emphasized that no matter where she went, she was able to participate in Mass each day, and that everywhere she found people involved in the Church and willing to talk about both the inspirations and the problems they found as believers in revolutionary Cuba. Some of them found it very difficult. "How can we send our children to schools where Marxism-Leninism is taught?" one mother asked Dorothy. "How can we take part in groups that are led by Marxists? How can we cooperate in such a society?"

Dorothy responded by describing the children of American black families who were insulted and jeered for entering schools that had previously been all white. One must be ready to withstand abuse and contempt, she said, and always be ready "to find concordances, as our Holy Father has urged, rather than to seek out heresies, to work as far as one can with the revolution, and always to be ready to give a reason for the faith that is in us." She carried with her two Catholic catechisms recently published on Cuban government presses, one for beginners, the other for more advanced students. Such booklets, she said, indicated that the government was seeking to fulfill its commitment to respect religious belief.

Wherever she went, Dorothy spoke about the Catholic Worker movement, its philosophy of work and its life of community with the poor and the oppressed. There had been no equivalent movement in Cuba, she realized. If only, she said, the Church would become less concerned with its own privileges and the comfort of the clergy and more concerned about the poor. So many priests "wear their lives away building ever bigger buildings and institutions while the family and the poor are left to the state to care for." Whenever religion ignores the urgent needs of the poor, offering them nothing but assurances of happiness after death, "then that religion is suspect."

Dorothy's Cuban diary left a number of her readers—some of them former co-workers—appalled. "Several of our old editors have accused us of giving up our pacifism," Dorothy noted. "What nonsense." She reaffirmed her opposition to violence, whether in war or the treatment of prisoners. "We are certainly not Marxist socialists nor do we believe in violent revolution. Yet we believe it is better to revolt, to fight as Castro did with his handful of men ... than to do nothing."

Nonetheless, her own way remained the nonviolent way of the Cross. Not the least part of her own suffering, she said, was the recognition "that so much suffering is unnecessary" and that so many who represent the Church "are shouting 'Lord, Lord' and yet denying Him in his poor, denying Him in their acceptance of the armies of the State." She pointed out that one of the unfortunate points of concordance existing between Marxists and most Catholics was that "both believe that there is nothing nobler for a young man than to bear arms for his country."

Dorothy's month-long stay in Cuba ended October 11, 1962, the very day when the first session of the Second Vatican Council was convened in St. Peter's Basilica in Rome, the vast church barely large enough to contain the flood of bishops, theologians and journalists. But within a few days world attention abruptly shifted from the Vatican to Cuba. American spy planes had discovered that Soviet medium-range missiles were being based in Cuba. Castro admitted it, saying they were there to deter any further U.S. invasions. On October 22, the U.S. government announced that it had placed Cuba under "naval quarantine." The United States demanded that the Soviets withdraw the missiles. American armed forces were put on alert, ready for war should the demand be ignored. War, possibly a world war fought with nuclear weapons, suddenly became an immediate possibility.

The fact that there was no war, it was learned only years later, was partly because of Pope John's personal intervention—his immediate attempt to find points of contact and agreement when accord seemed impossible.

In less than a week, a bargain was struck: Soviet missiles would be withdrawn from Cuba and the missile bases dismantled, an apparent "backing down" of the Russians before U.S. threats. Unseen by the world public was the parallel withdrawal of U.S. nuclear missiles based near the Soviet border in Turkey. At the same time, the United States made a secret pledge not to undertake or assist any further military attacks on Cuba.

A Death in the Family

One of the least visible figures at the Vatican Council was the Pope himself, who followed the proceedings by closed-circuit television in his private apartment overlooking St. Peter's Square. Despite failing health, he was able to carry on his various responsibilities, and he normally spoke to huge public audiences at least once a week. He was much engaged in writing an encyclical letter addressed not only to Catholics but to "every person of good will." *Pacem in Terris* (Peace on Earth) was signed and made public Holy Thursday, April 11, 1963. In it Pope John spoke eloquently of the "urgent demand that the arms race should cease." Peace between East and West, he said, was both possible and essential. Nuclear weapons should be entirely banned and states should enter into binding agreements to move step by step toward the elimination of other weapons. For centuries the Church had tolerated wars while trying to mitigate their worst consequences. John now declared that developments in weaponry were such that "it is irrational to argue that war can be considered a fit means to restore violated rights." Nor did the Pope agree that the work of peace should be entrusted only to the powerful and prominent: "There is an immense task incumbent on every person of good will, namely the task of restoring the relations of the human family in truth, in justice, in love, and in freedom." He recognized that those "endeavoring to restore the relations of social life ... are not many" but pleaded with them to persevere. He found comfort in the hope "that their number will increase, especially among those who believe." Engagement in peacemaking is not for an isolated minority but for everyone; it "is an imperative duty; it is a requirement of love."

Pacem in Terris, whose spirit and principles had long been anticipated by Dorothy, was still in the headlines when she sailed for Rome as one of fifty "Mothers for Peace." This was, she said, "a true pilgrimage, to the Holy City of Rome, to the head of the Church on earth ... to present ourselves as though the first fruit of his great encyclical, *Pacem in Terris*, to thank him, to pledge ourselves to the work for peace, and to ask, too, a more radical condemnation of the instruments of modern warfare." The mothers came from many countries and reflected the diversity of belief, religious and non-religious, found within the peace movement. A few were friends of Dorothy, including Hildegard Goss-Mayr from Vienna, the secretary of the International Fellowship of Reconciliation, and Hermene Evans and Marguerite Harris, both Americans, who together had provided Dorothy's ticket.

The group had hoped that a private audience with Pope John would be possible. Hildegard, Marguerite and Dorothy drafted a letter asking for such a meeting, explaining the group's purpose. It was given to one of the Pope's secretaries but there was no response. Other meetings did occur, however, including a long conversation with Cardinal Augustin Bea, head of the Vatican's Secretariat for Christian Unity, an intimate friend of Pope John's and a leading figure in the council. After the women had abandoned any hope for more personal contact with the Pope, they were invited to see him at a distance, during a public audience. "Finally there was a surge in the vast mob within St. Peter's Basilica," Dorothy wrote, "and a sudden silence followed by almost a roar of greeting. Borne aloft on his chair, the procession proceeded around the columns and then the Pope, blessing all, was conducted up to his throne where he sat while a list of all the pilgrim groups was read aloud. . . . And our pilgrimage was not even mentioned!" She imagined that no one had even made the Pope aware of the one pilgrimage group that had come in response to his peace encyclical. "But then the Pope began to speak and the words seemed directed to us." He expressed his gratitude and encouragement to the "Pilgrims for Peace." He thanked them for their message, said it brought comfort to his heart, blessed them and asked them to continue in their labors for peace. The women, wearing their large "Mothers for Peace" buttons, immediately became the attention point for others in the basilica. "It seemed too good to be true," Dorothy wrote, "and if those around us had not kept assuring us he was speaking to us, I would have considered it but a coincidence that he spoke as he did. Our message had reached him, impossible though it seemed."

Dorothy saw Pope John once again, May 22, the day before her departure. He was too weak from illness to leave his apartment (in earlier times these were rooms for servants) but stood at a window, leading the crowd in the recitation of the Angelus prayer. It was his next-to-last public appearance. He died June 3, just after Dorothy's arrival back in New York. For her and for a huge part of humanity, not only for Catholics, it was a death in the family.

Pope John's final days had been painful, Dorothy wrote in *The Catholic Worker*, and these sufferings, he made known, were offered by him as a prayer for the council and for world peace. "He had said, almost cheerfully," Dorothy continued, "that his bags were packed, and that he was ready to go, and that, after all, death was the beginning of a new life."

Angelo Roncalli — John — had been Pope only fifty-six months. But it was long enough. "He left us closer to God," one of the cardinals said when the council resumed, "and the world a better place to live." Certainly neither the Church nor the world was quite the same, which enraged some but moved many others to gratitude.

While in England that fall to speak at the annual meeting of the Pax Association, Dorothy visited the grave of Karl Marx at Highgate Cemetery, another man whose memory stirred both fury and gratitude. "The grave stands out because of its huge iron bust of Marx," Dorothy wrote her sister, Della. She described the mist; a crucifix standing opposite, the birds singing, and the fresh red roses on the Marx grave. Dorothy prayed especially for Marx's wife, Jenny, who for years had nothing to feed her family in their two-room Soho apartment but bread and potatoes. Several of their children had died of the consequences of destitution. Dorothy recalled how Jenny sought frantically for loans in order to buy the coffin for one daughter. She suffered several nervous breakdowns.

Dorothy's days in London included a boat ride up the Thames to Greenwich and a visit with Muriel Lester, former secretary of the International Fellowship of Reconciliation. Gandhi had stayed at her house of hospitality in the East End of London in 1931. Dorothy had a day with the Benedictine nuns at Stanbrook Abbey and another day in the ancient university town of Cambridge. A particular joy of her time in England was the opportunity to meet Donald Attwater, the great scholar and translator whose published work erected bridges between Christians of East and West, and between Christians of the modern world and their remarkable ancestors in the faith, the saints.

There was a refreshing stay with the Taena Community near Gloucester. Here twelve adults, twenty-three children, thirty-five cows, forty-five sheep and eighty chickens shared one hundred thirty acres. Dorothy stayed in a stone farmhouse that stood on sixteenth-century foundations "with no, God forbid, central heating." In her column, she described an animated discussion with the children of the family about the annual bonfire which consumes the effigy of the bomb-planting revolutionist, Guy Fawkes. Days before the burning, Dorothy found the straw-stuffed figure at home in the living room, man-sized, with a clown face, lolling in an easy chair. "Rebecca sits on his lap and Rachael wags his head, but he will not be treated so kindly next week. . . . It occurred to me to be shocked by all this, and I suggested that the children have a trial and pardon the dynamiter, but they will have none of it."

A Single Condemnation

Dorothy made two more trips to Rome.

In September 1965 she sailed with Eileen Egan, a close friend who directed the work of Catholic Relief Services in south Asia and who was a founder of Pax (later the U.S. section of Pax Christi International). They brought with them several hundred copies of a special issue of *The Catholic Worker* on "The Council and the Bomb." The third and final session of the Vatican Council was about to open. Its agenda included completion of a text, passages of which had aroused active opposition from the American military establishment: Schema 13, as it was called in the drafting stage, finally published as the *Pastoral Constitution on the Church in the Modern World.*

Once again Dorothy was part of a community of women, this time only twenty and all Catholics. They had committed themselves to a ten-day fast expressing, Dorothy said, "our prayer and our hope" that the council would issue "a clear statement, 'Put away thy sword.'" They hoped the council would endorse active nonviolence as an appropriate means of struggle for social justice, give their support to those who refused to do military service, and condemn weapons of mass destruction.

After several days of meeting with bishops and others active in the council, Dorothy enjoyed an evening meal at Il Scoglio, a noted Roman restaurant. "I felt rather guilty at prefacing a penitential fast in this way," she confessed to readers of her column, "but Eileen reminded me that, after all, Lent was prefaced by *carnivale.*"

The next morning, after an eastern rite Mass at St. Peter's, Dorothy made her way to the Cenacle on Piazza Priscilla at the edge of Rome where the women had gathered for their fast. Each day that followed began with an early Mass. Times of common prayer, reading and conversation were scattered through the day. There was a daily lecture and at 6 P.M. a doctor visited to be sure of each faster's well-being. The only nourishment taken was water.

Dorothy had fasted before and expected hunger, headaches and nausea, but instead experienced a deeper and different suffering than she had ever known before. "I had offered my fast in part for the victims of famine all over the world, and it seemed to me that I had very special pains . . . a kind

I had never known before which seemed to pierce to the very marrow of my bones as I lay down at night." She was sixty-eight and accustomed to arthritic pain "which one accepts as part of age." But in these pains she found "an intimation of the hunger of the world." Rest eluded her at night. In the day she was refreshed by knitting, reading, and conversation with visitors—some of them bishops and abbots—who had heard of the fast despite the fasters' avoidance of all publicity.

On the night of October 10, the fast ended, as it had begun, with prayer. Hard though it had been for Dorothy, she regarded it as a "widow's mite, a few loaves and fishes. May we try harder to do more in the future."

She made no claim that this almost invisible act of witness had influenced the council, or that it had been more important than the public exhibition on nonviolence and peacemaking that had been set up for the bishops by the organizers of the fast, the Community of the Ark, the European Gandhian movement. But she was convinced that prayer and fasting had a power that even believers rarely imagine. In a hidden but significant way, the fasting women had participated in the work of the council.

She had reason to rejoice in December when, on the next-to-last day of the council, the *Pastoral Constitution on the Church in the Modern World* was passed, complete with its many controversial passages, by the overwhelming majority of the bishops. The text included the only specific condemnation produced by the Second Vatican Council: "Every act of war directed to the indiscriminate destruction of whole cities or vast areas with their inhabitants is a crime against God and humanity, which merits firm and unequivocal condemnation." Emphasizing the role of conscience, the bishops called on states to make legal provision for those "who, for reasons of conscience, refuse to bear arms, provided that they agree to serve the human community in some other way." Those who renounce violence altogether, seeking a more just and compassionate society by nonviolent means, were honored: "We cannot fail to praise those who renounce the use of violence in vindication of their rights and who resort to methods of defense which are otherwise available to weaker parties too, provided this can be done without injury to the rights and duties of others or to the community itself." Those who, in the name of obedience, obey commands which condemn the innocent and defenseless were described as "criminal," while those who disobey such corrupt commands merit "supreme commendation."

If the final document contained numerous indications of compromise and was a far cry from the Sermon on the Mount, still the council text was a vindication for Dorothy and the Catholic Worker movement. Thus it was hardly surprising that when Dorothy was next in Rome, in October 1967, for the International Congress of the Laity, she was there as an honored and well-cared-for guest. Of the Americans present, she was one of two— the other an astronaut—invited to receive Communion from the hands of Pope Paul VI during the final Mass of the Congress in St. Peter's.

What had she felt about this privilege, a journalist asked.

"I could think nothing, feel nothing, but only to say a most heartfelt prayer for Pope Paul, who had been ill and who looked that morning as though he were under a great strain." She prayed for others as well, she recalled, including "all those nonviolent ones who are in prison today, for their conscientious objection to this terrible Vietnam war in which we are now engaged."

A Time of Burning Children

As the issue of war was being debated in the exquisite Renaissance environment of St. Peter's in Rome, war was being fought in Vietnam. In 1965, "Americanization" of the war began with U.S. bombing of North Vietnam and the landing of 3,500 Marine combat troops at Danang in the South. The number of U.S. troops climbed to 510,000 within three years. To many it seemed that a daily battle was being fought between David and Goliath, as defenseless hamlets were destroyed by jets and helicopters. For every insurgent Vietnamese soldier killed, it was estimated that ten or twenty ordinary civilians died, most often children and the aged, those least quick or skilled in finding shelter. "Anti-personnel" weapons were developed which implanted tiny bits of razor-edged metal or plastic in their victims. Napalm was widely used: gasoline chemically treated so that, while burning, it clung to the skin like glue. Vietnam, wrote the Jesuit priest Daniel Berrigan, had become "the land of burning children."

Dorothy had only recently returned from her fast in Rome when a death by burning occurred within the Catholic Worker community. At 5:20 A.M., November 9, 1965, Roger LaPorte sat in the street before the United States Mission to the United Nations two miles north of the Catholic Worker house, poured gasoline on himself, struck a match, and became a pillar of fire in the darkness of night. "I am a Catholic Worker," he said before lapsing into a coma at a nearby hospital. "I did this as a religious action. I am anti-war, all wars." Before his death twenty-two hours later, he regained consciousness. "I want to live," he told a Carmelite priest who heard his last confession. "He made the most devout act of contrition I have ever heard," the priest said afterward. "His voice was strong and he meant every word."

Only a few weeks earlier, Roger had been present with other young volunteers from the Catholic Worker for a peace rally at Union Square where several pacifists burned their draft registration cards as an act of civil disobedience. One of them was Tom Cornell, co-secretary of the Catholic Peace Fellowship who had previously been managing editor of *The Catholic Worker*. Dorothy addressed the crowd in support of Tom and the others, pointing out to them that, in advocating and supporting such gestures of resistance, she too was breaking the law. Such actions were necessary, she said, in order to make others aware of the "immorality of war." As she spoke, supporters of the war across the street chanted, "Moscow Mary! Moscow Mary!" When the draft cards were ignited, their chant became, "Burn yourselves, not your draft cards!"

Roger burned himself.

"It has always been the teaching of the Catholic Church," Dorothy wrote in the days following Roger's death, "that suicide is a sin, but mercy and loving-kindness dictate another judgment." She noted that normally those who take their own lives are temporarily unbalanced, possibly insane, and thus can be absolved from their guilt. But there was no indication of mental illness in Roger, she went on. He had been an honor student who had entered the seminary and then tried the monastic life before coming to the Catholic Worker in 1963, where he had devoted himself wholeheartedly to the poor and sick while still carrying on his studies. What he did "must be spoken of in a far deeper context [than despair or mental illness]. It is not only that many youth and students throughout the country are deeply sensitive to the sufferings of the world. They have a keen sense that they must be responsible and make a profession of their faith that things do not have to go on as they always have — that men are capable of laying down their lives for others." She recalled the revolutionary in Ignazio Silone's novel, *Bread and Wine*, who risked capture and execution by leaving his hiding place to write slogans of dissent on public walls in fascist Italy. Someone scolded him for endangering himself in order to make such insignificant gestures. The dissenter responded, "The Land of Propaganda is built on unanimity. If anyone says, 'No,' the spell is broken and the public order is endangered."

Roger had used his own flesh as a wall to bear that message, to cry a No that might be heard throughout America. "In forty-eight hours last week," Dorothy reminded her readers, "there were six massive air strikes in Vietnam. There were more killed on both sides last week than at any time since the war began." While the young and innocent died, others living in safety grew wealthy from the war. She cited a headline she had noticed a few days earlier in *The Wall Street Journal*:

VIETNAM SPURS PLANNING FOR BIG RISE IN OUTLAYS
FOR MILITARY HARDWARE
SPENDING ON TANKS, COPTERS, OTHER GEAR MAY DOUBLE

The *Journal* article seemed to rejoice in the recent U.S. commitment to a more active combat role in Vietnam. This promised to give "added zip for the nation's economy," the *Journal* predicted, by funneling "billions into pocketbooks in many parts of the country."

"There is something satanic about this kind of writing," said Dorothy. "On the other hand, witness Roger LaPorte. He embraced voluntary poverty and came to the Catholic Worker because he did not wish to profit in this booming economy of which *The Wall Street Journal* speaks so gloatingly. He was giving himself to the poor and the destitute, serving tables, serving the sick. . . . And now he is dead—dead by his own hand, everyone will say, a suicide."

Dorothy saw Roger instead as a "victim soul" who had been constantly searching for ways to offer his life for others, trying to take to himself "the sufferings that we as a nation are inflicting upon a small country and its people." He was not driven by despair or the hatred of life but rather by compassion and an anguished awareness of those who were being burned, far from our sight, in the villages of Vietnam. Yes, it was a "sad and terrible act, but all of us around the Catholic Worker know that Roger's intent was to love God and his brother."

The 1960s was a decade with many "sad and terrible" events—invasions, wars, assassinations, the murder of civil rights workers—but also a decade of extraordinary breakthroughs: the Vatican Council, *Pacem in Terris*, and the passage by Congress of the Civil Rights Act. It was also a decade of immense social dislocation and experiments in new life styles, ranging from attempts at community life to engagement with psychedelic drugs. In San Francisco, a rundown section called Haight-Ashbury became a battered mecca for flower children, while the Catholic Worker's neighborhood in New York—the East Village—acquired a similar reputation. Thousands of young people, whose parents had been models of hard work, good behavior, success and patriotism, found themselves estranged from America's political and economic structures, which seemed the source of high-technology murder in Vietnam. In a wide variety of ways, young men found ways to evade the draft—some by obtaining student deferments, some by hiding, and some by leaving the country. Many became conscientious objectors, a legal option for those of religious motivation who were opposed in principle to all war. They did two years of alternative service, usually helping in hospitals. A smaller number who often would have qualified as conscientious objectors refused to seek any special recognition or exemption from the draft boards and often spent two or three years in prison. (Dorothy was close to people in both groups, though her heart was especially with the draft resisters; draft-age men in the Catholic Worker movement during the Vietnam war tended to end up in prison.)

Hundreds of thousands of people took part in demonstrations, teach-ins, vigils, picket lines and other acts of protest. Never in American history had so many been engaged in public opposition to their country's military activities.

In 1965, the Catholic Worker, in combination with the Fellowship of Reconciliation, gave birth to the Catholic Peace Fellowship, which concentrated on educational work directed at Catholic students, educators and pastors. Its booklet, "Catholics and Conscientious Objection," went through edition after edition; during the Vietnam war, 150,000 were printed. By the latter 1960s, the Catholic Peace Fellowship was often counseling, in person or by letter, fifty conscientious objectors and draft resisters a week.

Many found that the refusal to do military service was only a first step and looked for ways to impede the war by active, nonviolent resistance. Some of the actions that emerged were intentionally shocking and controversial, even within the peace movement itself. "Let us burn paper instead of children," Daniel Berrigan advised. Catholic Workers such as Chris Kern, David Miller and Tom Cornell had burned their own draft cards. Then in April 1968, nine Catholics, including Daniel and Philip Berrigan, entered the draft board offices in the town of Catonsville, Maryland, took out the files of those classified as draft eligible, and burned the papers in an adjacent parking lot with homemade napalm. In the early fall, a group of fourteen, including several associated with the Catholic Worker movement, took similar records from all nine boards of the city of Milwaukee, burning them in a park while reading from the Gospel and praying until they were put under arrest.

"It is mid-October and the weather is still warm," Dorothy wrote soon after the Milwaukee action. "The maples and the oaks and the sumac are brilliant. ... If only there were not the radio! The news of bloody death and destruction at the other end of the world, in the name of defense. ... It is in the light of this anguish that one can understand the attempt made by the Catonsville Nine and the Milwaukee Fourteen, amongst whom so many are our friends, to suffer with these fellow human beings so devastated by war and famine. These men — priests and laymen — have offered themselves as a living sacrifice, as hostages. They have offered the most precious gift apart from life itself, their freedom, as well as the prayer and fasting they have done behind bars, for these others" — both the Vietnamese and the young Americans "being enslaved in our immoral wars."

Despite her support for those imprisoned for burning draft records, Dorothy found the destruction of property a difficult, troubling issue. She agreed that Jesus had given a similar example in destroying the stands of the money-changers in the temple in Jerusalem. But she also said that we ought not do to others what we would not have them do to us. She worried too that less dramatic efforts to end the war would be denigrated and judged less valuable than actions that risked long prison sentences. Early in 1969, she reminded her readers that peacemaking most often took quite ordinary forms. "The thing is to recognize that not all are called, not all have the vocation, to demonstrate in this way, to fast, to endure the pain and the long, drawn out, nerve-wracking suffering of prison life. We do what we can, and the whole field of the works of mercy is open to us. ... All work, whether building, increasing food production, running credit unions, working in factories that produce for human needs, working in the handicrafts — all these things can come under the heading of the works of mercy, which are the opposite of the works of war."

The dimension of penance was essential to any work of social healing, Dorothy emphasized, but penance isn't only found in the deprivations of prison. "It is a penance to work, to give oneself to others, to endure the pin-pricks of community life. One could certainly say on many occasions, 'Give me a thorough, frank, outgoing war, rather than the sneak attacks, stabs in the back, sparring, detracting, defaming, hand-to-hand jockeying for position that go on in offices and "good works" of all kinds, another and miserable petty kind of war.' ... So let us rejoice in our own petty sufferings and thank God we have a little penance to offer."

Yet there were those who were called to acts of resistance that could result in prison and even injury and death. She compared Daniel Berrigan to an earlier Jesuit, St. Edmund Campion, who had been an underground priest when Catholicism was outlawed in England and who had been tortured to death during the reign of the first Queen Elizabeth. She thought too of the example of Martin Luther King, "a man of the deepest and most profound spiritual insights," who had so often been jailed, whose home had been repeatedly bombed, who had almost died of a knife wound, and who was finally shot down in Memphis on the eve of Good Friday, 1968.

Those who gave up their freedom and risked their lives, Dorothy argued, were not disobedient. They were obedient to the way of the Cross. They were obedient to the commandment not to kill. It was not they who should be accused. "I accuse," wrote Dorothy, "the government itself, and all of us, of these mass murders in Vietnam, this destruction of villages, this wiping out of peoples, the kidnaping, torture, rape and killings that have been disclosed to us. ... Reparation is needed. We must do penance for what we have done to our brothers. ... But meanwhile in this hushed room there is prayer, for strength to know and to love and to find out what to do and set our hands to useful work that will contribute to peace, not to war."

Dorothy also challenged the American bishops for their role in Vietnam, which in the early years of the war mainly ranged from passive to active support. Probably the most outspoken supporter was Cardinal Spellman who, while visiting U.S. troops in Vietnam, told them they were engaged in a struggle for civilization.

"I sit in the presence of the Blessed Sacrament," Dorothy wrote from the chapel at the Catholic Worker farm, "and wrestle for peace in the bitterness of my soul. ... " She noted that the hardest people to love are usually not far away but close at hand, even in one's own religious community, one's Church. She wondered if "these princes of the Church" are not blinded to Christ's presence in "the enemy" because of their terror of the enemy. In Cardinal Spellman she noted genuine courage in his annual Christmas visits to American troops, not only in Vietnam but places all over the world. "But oh God, what are all these Americans, so many of them Christians, doing all over the world, so far from their own shores?"

In 1967, the year she asked this question, one of the soldiers in Vietnam was her grandson Eric.

She recalled that Cardinal Spellman, ignoring papal appeals for a negotiated peace, had called for total victory in the war. "Words are strong and powerful as bombs," she commented, "powerful as napalm. How much the government counts on those words, pays for those words to exalt our own way of life, to build up fear of the enemy. . . . Love casts out fear, but we have to get over the fear in order to get close enough to love those we fear." She wished that everyone would read the Book of Hosea, which is so emphatic about God's steadfast love not only for the Jews, the chosen people, but for everyone. "We are all one, all one body, Chinese, Russians, Vietnamese, and He has *commanded* us to love one another."

Farmworkers

The first *Catholic Worker* article on farm workers appeared in 1934. Beginning in 1965, and for more than a decade, it was a rare issue which failed to speak about the farm workers' struggle to unionize themselves. Attempts in earlier years had been crushed so effectively that farm workers were considered the best example of the labor strata that could not be organized: many of the workers moved with the crops, had no community roots, had no influence with legislators, and were invisible to the press and public. Growers had easily crushed the few strikes that had been organized in the past. But in 1962, Cesar Chavez, a Mexican American who had grown up on the fields, ignored much advice and founded the National Farm Workers Association. His only economic base was his $1,200 savings. By 1964, he had signed up a thousand members and been joined by several co-workers. In 1965, the union won a pay raise for grape workers on one California ranch. In the fall, a strike — *huelga* — by grape workers on other ranches sought to extend the first small victory. In 1966, a much bigger gain was celebrated when Schenley Industries not only gave a pay raise but signed a contract, the first such contract ever negotiated in the history of American farm labor. By this time, a nationwide network had been built up which appealed effectively for consumer boycotts: over a period of years, successive boycotts removed iceberg lettuce, table grapes, raisins and (among other labels) Gallo wine from hundreds of thousands of homes and institutions. Rejoicing over the Schenley contract, one worker wrote to Dorothy, "Now we have rest rooms and a place to wash our hands."

While Dorothy was supportive of any union effort, Cesar was of special importance to her because of his emphasis on his religious faith and his insistance on nonviolence. "We have recognized," Dorothy wrote in her column in 1967, "that the problem of agriculture is insoluble without tapping the deep religious instincts for patience and perseverance of the people."

In April, Cesar came to visit Dorothy and to see the Catholic Worker community in New York. "He looks just like his pictures," Dorothy noted, "perhaps even younger, with straight black hair, face browned by the sun, and brown as an Indian's is brown." They had in common a deep devotion to Mary, the mother of Jesus. "When he saw the picture of Our Lady of

Guadalupe which has been hanging on our walls for so long that it is dark with age, he immediately left his seat at the table and stood before it a few moments before we began to talk." Banners of Our Lady of Guadalupe had been prominent in farm worker marches. He told her about the truck-loads of food and clothing being sent down regularly by the Catholic Worker community in the San Francisco Bay area.

"When finally farm workers are organized in one small town after another," Dorothy wrote about their common vision, "and all together begin to feel their strength in the largest of all United States' industries, agriculture, they may begin to have a vision of the kind of society where the workers will be owners — of their own homes, a few acres, and eventually of large holdings in the form of cooperatives." She suggested to Cesar that Israel's *kibbutzim* might be models for agricultural development in the United States.

In May 1969, Dorothy went west by bus on a speaking trip that brought her to Delano, a town in the San Joaquin Valley in central California, then the headquarters of the farm worker campaign. "My shoes are covered with dust and I am down at the heels indeed," she wrote back to New York. A priest met her at the Delano bus terminal and took her to Cesar and Helen Chavez's small house. Once inside the door she found a picture of Gandhi on the wall identical to one at the Catholic Worker's 1st Street house in New York — and a picture of Our Lady of Guadalupe. It was in this house that Cesar had fasted for twenty-five days in 1968, an act of penance for striker violence that renewed the union's commitment to nonviolence.

The day after her arrival, Dorothy took part in a memorial Mass for Robert Kennedy. "It was the first anniversary of his death," she wrote, "and Chavez will always remember that Kennedy came and broke bread with him as he ended his fast. He considered him a *compañero* in a very deep sense." Dorothy was asked by Cesar to read the Epistle, and after the Mass he called on her to speak. "The best thing about this," she said, "was that it gave me a view of the packed hall with the beautiful dark faces of the Filipinos and the Mexicans, men, women and children, the seats all filled, and the aisles, yet no one restless. They broke out now and then in a crescendo of applause which became faster and faster clapping of hands and stamping of feet which died down as suddenly as it flared up. And there were the shouts of *Viva la huelga*, *Viva la causa*, over and over again."

Dorothy took part in the dawn picketing of one of the fields and was nearly run down when a car, in a sudden burst of speed, swerved toward her. Despite her years, she was agile enough to leap back to safety. The tire tracks were shown to a sheriff, who had previously been taking down the name of a striker who had ventured into the grape field to talk to the pickers. "The sheriff was perfunctory about both complaints," Dorothy wrote. The driver wasn't arrested. Dorothy noted the many strikers who were not simply endangered but injured. One striker had been cut on his face with grape scissors, another kicked in the ribs and beaten by a grower, and still another kicked in the face and body by a foreman. Dorothy wrote their names and the details of what had happened to them, and quoted a proverb of the strikers: "We have to sacrifice to deserve."

It was a beautiful morning, with singing birds offering "such a paean of praise to their Maker." But the fierce heat was quick in coming. "There was no breeze and such a dust haze that one could not see the mountains, though they were nearby." Dorothy watched the workers—strike-breakers—in the field, thinning leaves, tossing aside defective grapes, putting bunches of good grapes in paper-lined boxes. "I saw children in the field, helping their parents." The pay, one of the strikers told her, was $1.10 an hour, with a penny extra for each vine thinned. A good worker, doing a six-day week, could thin three hundred vines. But the striker recalled trying to collect the extra three dollars one week and instead being threatened by the grower with a rifle.

"Remember these things," Dorothy asked readers of *The Catholic Worker*, "you whose mouth waters for table grapes. Remember the boycott and help the strikers. ... Their struggle has gone on for years now. It is the first breakthrough to achieve some measure of Justice for these poorest and most beloved of God's children."

Late in 1971, after a stay with the Catholic Worker community in Los Angeles, Dorothy was with Cesar again. The threats on his life were such that the union had put a high wire fence around his house. Cesar was accompanied by two German shepherds (Boycott and Huelga) wherever he went, and an unarmed but large bodyguard. Though head of the union, he continued to receive the same pay provided every worker on the union staff: room and board, travel money when needed, and $5 a week. They renewed their conversation about long-range visions, when workers would no longer be "hired hands" but would have a share in the land they worked. In their discussion of the violence the union was experiencing daily from its opponents, it impressed Dorothy that Cesar never spoke of "enemies" but only of "adversaries." He had refused to dehumanize the growers.

In the column describing her 1971 stay with the farm workers, Dorothy tried to respond to several critical letters that had been received from contributors who wanted to be sure that their gifts would be used to feed the hungry and not to publish "propaganda" and social criticism. "Why," such readers asked Dorothy, "do you give so much attention in *The Catholic Worker* to such matters as the condition of workers, unions, boycotts?"

"Let me say," Dorothy replied, "that the sight of a line of men waiting for food, dirty, ragged, obviously sleeping out in empty buildings, is something that I will never get used to. It is a deep hurt and suffering that food is often all we have to give. Our houses will not hold any more men and women, nor do we have workers to care for them. Nor are there enough alternatives or services to care for them. They are the wounded of the class struggle, men who have built the railroads, worked in the mines, on ships, and steel mills. They are men — and women too — from prison and mental hospitals. They are often simply the unemployed.

"But bread lines are not enough, hospices are not enough. I know that we will always have men on the road. But we need communities of work, land for the landless, true farming communes, cooperatives and credit unions. There is much that is wild, prophetic and holy about our work. . . . The heart hungers for the new social order wherein justice dwelleth."

It was this longing for such a new social order that drew her toward Cesar. It was because of this hope that the Catholic Worker could never simply be a movement of hospitality for the victims of what Dorothy at times described as "this filthy, rotten system."

Dorothy's sense of identification with the farm worker struggle resulted in her last stay in prison. In the summer of 1973, Joan Baez invited Dorothy to spend a week with the Institute for the Study of Nonviolence in California. By the time she arrived, however, a California judge had forbidden farm worker picket lines. "My path was clear," Dorothy wrote. "The UFW has everything that belongs to a new social order." She decided to take part in the prohibited picket lines. On August 1, after rising at 2 A.M., she picketed through the day at several vineyards, facing lines of police armed with clubs and guns. She occasionally rested on her folding chair-cane, a much used item in her later years. "We talked to the police," she wrote, "pleading with them to lay down their weapons." She told them she planned to return on the following day and would read aloud the Sermon on the Mount.

The next day, after a night with the nurses at one of the farm worker clinics that the union had opened, she was up at 4 A.M. and at a meeting before dawn where Cesar spoke about the latest arrests. "We set out in cars to picket the area where the big and small growers had united to get the injunction. Three police buses arrived some time later and we were warned to disperse. When we refused, we were ushered into buses and brought to this 'industrial farm' (which they do not like us to call a jail or prison, though we are under lock and key and our barracks surrounded by barbed wire). Here we are, ninety-nine women and fifty men, including thirty nuns and two priests." They were charged with "remaining present at the place of a riot, rout and unlawful assembly" from which they refused to disperse despite lawful warning.

Bob Fritch's photo of Dorothy, sitting on her chair-cane, in calm discussion with a crowd of heavily armed police, hit the nation's press and is probably the photo of Dorothy that has been most widely seen. She looks like a mother patiently admonishing children about war toys.

While crucial negotiations involving the UFW were going on through the night, the nuns organized a prayer vigil with two-hour shifts. The Mexican women prayed the rosary with their arms outstretched, as if themselves with Christ on the cross. "Our barracks were alive with prayer," Dorothy reported.

During the days, there were seminars. Dorothy led one on labor history. Another prisoner, a great lover of St. Thomas and St. Augustine, taught about rhetoric. "I tried to understand what rhetoric really means," Dorothy admitted, "and she explained, but I cannot remember now."

On August 8, Daniel Ellsberg and Joan Baez came to visit. "Joan sang to us a most poignant prison song, which tore your heart. "

On August 13, after nearly two weeks on the prison farm, the charges were dropped and the prisoners — industrial farmers — were freed. Dorothy surprised the warden by her refusal to return her prison dress. In their gratitude for her presence with them, the others arrested with her had signed it and made it a gift. "This is state property, Miss Day," she was told. "You can't keep it." "My friends have written their names on it,"she replied. "They gave it to me and I won't give it up." The authorities relented and Dorothy kept the dress.

In Fresno that night, in a park across from the courthouse, the farm workers celebrated Mass. They rightly felt that a small victory had been won, though it was another two years before state laws were passed that allowed farm workers to freely choose their own union representation in secret-ballot elections. The great majority chose the UFW.

It wasn't until 1978 that the UFW was secure enough to retire its major weapon, the nationwide consumer boycott. By then the UFW was a secure national structure representing farm workers in various states, from California to Florida, though still only a minor percentage of farm workers were union members and the grower fight to prevent agriculture unions was far from over.

"The human cost in personal and family life of establishing the UFW was an incalculable price paid by the legions of dedicated, idealistic and sometimes driven people who made the union a reality," the lead article in the February 1978 *Catholic Worker* commented. The writer, Marion Moses, expressed her hope that the UFW would never lose its original values and become just one more selfish labor bureaucracy. There were still hundreds of thousands of unorganized farm workers in need of a union "hungering and thirsting after justice."

Further Travels

"On pilgrimage" in January 1970, Dorothy's travels took her to Utah (for Ammon Hennacy's funeral), then on to Florida, Georgia and Michigan. A nurse at the Detroit Catholic Worker community noticed Dorothy's difficulty in breathing and took her to a nearby hospital. "This is a case of heart failure," Dorothy wrote that night in her journal. "Water in my lungs, hardening of arteries, enlarged heart and so on were responsible for the pains in my chest and shortness of breath, which makes me sit gasping for five minutes after I walk a block or have to hurry or am oppressed by haste, urgency, etc." The hospital visit went unmentioned in her column.

Despite the news, she pressed on to Boston before returning home, then later in the year undertook the most extensive trip of her life: a round-the-world journey that brought her to Australia, Hong Kong, India, Tanzania, Rome and England. Her traveling companion was her long-time friend, Eileen Egan.

At the airport in Calcutta, Mother Teresa met them and garlanded them with fresh flowers before taking them to the Missionary Sisters' hospice for the dying in the heart of the city. During her days with the community, Dorothy had an opportunity to speak to the novices. She stressed a theme that was central to both their order and to the Catholic Worker movement: Christ remains with us not only through the Mass but in the "distressing disguise" of the poor. To live with the poor is a contemplative vocation, for it is to live in the constant presence of Jesus. The novices were astonished at Dorothy's accounts of her arrests and times in jail. "They understood going to prison for truth and liberation, as Gandhi had done," wrote Eileen, an old friend of Mother Teresa. "Now they were hearing it in a specifically Christian context, that of the work of mercy of visiting the prisoner by entering prison."

After Dorothy's talk, Mother Teresa pinned on Dorothy's dress the black cross with the figure of Christ worn by all the professed members of the order. No other lay person had been honored by Mother Teresa in this way. It was another event about which Dorothy was silent in her column.

Dorothy and Eileen went on to Dar-es-Salaam, to which members of the Maryknoll missionary congregation had invited them. From the air, Dorothy was thrilled to see the great mountain, Kilimanjaro, the highest point in

Africa, but what impressed her still more was the effort going on in Tanzania to develop a gentle socialism that respected the villages. She noted that Tanzania was the first state in Africa to provide exemption for conscientious objectors to military service.

Still ignoring her weak heart, Dorothy joined Nina Polcyn, a friend from Chicago, in going with a tour group to eastern Europe in July 1971. The stops included Poland, Bulgaria and Hungary, but the largest part of the journey was in the Soviet Union. To Dorothy it was "Holy Mother Russia" to which she had been drawn by years of reading, by the icons that had become a part of her prayer life, and by several friendships. One of the friends was a Russian exile, Helene Iswolsky, teacher of Russian language, literature, history and spirituality at Fordham University, and founder of the Third Hour, an ecumenical group in which Dorothy and W. H. Auden participated. Helene Iswolsky eventually made the Catholic Worker her home, living in a room at the Tivoli farm amid her books and icons.

In Leningrad—today St. Petersburg—Dorothy was joined by another friend who taught Russian in New York and who was in the city for a summer course at a language institute. Together they did some exploring on the side, the high point of which was at the Alexander Nevsky Monastery on the Neva River. Adjacent to the monastery was the cemetery where many writers, artists and composers were buried. Dorothy prayed at the grave of her beloved Dostoyevsky, mentor for more than half a century, so many of whose fictional characters she spoke of with the familiarity of friendship.

Within the monastery walls they found an Orthodox seminary and a "working church" (in contrast to a museum church). "It was in the middle of the week, so we did not expect a service, or even that the church would be open. But as we passed the rear of the church in our exploration of the grounds, we saw seated on some boxes a row of little old ladies, drably dressed and with babushkas over their heads, murmuring together like a row of birds. A nun joined them and my friend asked about a service. Yes, at five Vespers would start and the church door would be opened. So we too sat and waited, and it was good to sit.

"It was a long service, but there was a good choir of mixed voices and some beautiful singing." Dorothy was ashamed that because of her arthritis, she had to sit part of the time on her cane-chair. She recalled that in the old times even the czar had to stand throughout the liturgy. During the service, the old were joined by the young, including parents with children in their arms. "We left before the service was over and by that time the church was full of lighted candles and the smoke of incense. We too venerated the icons and went away happy that we had had the opportunity to praise God."

"The life of the spirit goes on," Dorothy told her co-workers in New York, despite unimaginable suffering. She reminded them that a third of the population of Leningrad, a million people, had died—many of starvation and the cold — during the city's 872-day siege during the Second World War. "Now you see a religious revival among the young, many of whom are being baptized and bringing their friends to belief with them."

She recalled the great suffering that Russian believers have experienced since the Revolution, the times of "awful desecration of churches and icons trampled underfoot, acts expressing the hatred of religion when it collaborated so closely with the government."

Dorothy offered occasional troubling moments to the government at officially arranged meetings. While expressing gratitude for the care being given churches and icons in the modern Soviet Union, and the rarity of "crude expressions of atheism," she was distressed at the harsh treatment of Alexander Solzhenitsyn. She compared him to Dostoyevsky and Tolstoy. "Perhaps it was my tribute and my expressions of regret at the treatment of this great Russian that caused the meeting to break up."

In Moscow, Dorothy prayed the Psalms each day while looking out a window that offered a view of four churches whose many brilliantly colored onion domes were shining in the summer sky. The most exuberant church in view was St. Basil's, which dominated Red Square. While she knew that it was now only a museum, she saw it even in this capacity as an invitation to faith. "Who knows what the effect will be on millions of children who are guided through such churches, even the ones that are museums today? 'The world will be saved by beauty,' Dostoyevsky wrote in *The Idiot.*"

On the same square was Lenin's Tomb, to which so many people from every corner of the Soviet Union came each day on pilgrimage, waiting in line for hours before entering the austere marble structure by the Kremlin wall. Dorothy joined the procession, at last finding herself in a room lit with a soft blue light. Lenin's body rested on a stone slab. "The silence was rather awesome," she said. "I stopped a moment to make the Sign of the Cross and to say a prayer for this man who brought such upheaval into the world."

She prayed again at the nearby Tretyakov Gallery, a museum housing many of the masterpieces of Russian art. Most beloved to Dorothy were Rublev's icon of the Holy Trinity and the ancient Vladimir icon of the Mother of God. Dorothy stood before the image — the face of the infant Jesus pressed gently against his mother's worried face, a work legend had attributed to St. Luke — and thanked God that "the Russians are not following the example of the West, where we seem to be trying to obliterate devotion to Our Lady." Reproductions of the Vladimir icon, or similar icons inspired by it, remain places of prayer and devotion in every Russian Orthodox home and church.

"These icons," Dorothy told the community at Tivoli when she was home in August, "have such tenderness and beauty. They make you think of all mothers, all children. They help us to overcome all violence and hatred."

Life in a Railroad Station

Flying to Calcutta after a brief stop-over in Hong Kong, Dorothy's plane had passed directly over Vietnam. From the air, Dorothy could see no evidence of the war that year after year was claiming so many Vietnamese and American lives, while bringing many participants in the Catholic Worker movement to prison.

It was not until after the Vietnam war that the Catholic Worker community became fully aware of how much attention its many years of anti-war activities had generated in the Federal Bureau of Investigation. Following an application from the staff in New York, made under the terms of the Freedom of Information Act, sections of the FBI files were received bit by bit in the latter 1970s. Altogether 575 pages were delivered, many of them censored, while other pages were withheld "for reasons of national security." The FBI investigation stretched from the Second World War to the war in Vietnam. The file was opened when the Bureau received a tip in 1940 about a radical front in New York the informer referred to as "The Dorothy Day Art Studio." In due course the FBI became aware that there was no art studio but a soup kitchen, and the proprietor was worth keeping an eye on. On April 3, 1941, six months before U.S. entry into the war, J. Edgar Hoover filed a memorandum with the Special Defense Unit of the Justice Department recommending that Dorothy Day "be considered for custodial detention in the event of national emergency."

The last major entry in the file concerned Dorothy's speech at Union Square in 1965 in support of Tom Cornell and others who were burning their draft cards that day to protest conscription and the war in Vietnam. By this time thoughts of detaining her had cooled, though it was clear she was liable for prosecution for having advocated a violation of the Selective Service Act.

During the Vietnam war, however, the government agency that was most fascinated by the Catholic Worker was the Internal Revenue Service, the nation's tax collector — and, from the Catholic Worker point of view, chief fund-raiser for war.

The IRS found the Catholic Worker an enthralling, peculiar object. No one, including Dorothy Day, received any salary. Yet it couldn't be regarded as a convent or monastery: no one wore special clothes or took any vows.

Nor was it a "charity" in any usual sense of the word: what was given away, Dorothy always stressed, was as much a work of justice as charity. In any event, what charity was identified with protest or spoke of revolution?

In April 1972, during a period of military escalation in Vietnam, an IRS letter addressed to *The Catholic Worker* demanded payment of $296,359 in what was described as unpaid taxes plus fines and interest. Dorothy wondered whether this was the beginning of a process that would lead her back to prison. At least it seemed quite likely that it could mean the confiscation of the Worker bank account ("never very large," she noted) and all community property, especially the house on First Street and the farm at Tivoli. Dorothy struggled to imagine what could be done, if worse came to worst, for the forty adults and twelve children then in residence at Tivoli, plus another crowd of adults in New York who were packed into First Street "like sardines." "I can only trust that this crisis will pass," Dorothy wrote in the May issue, "that some way will be found to avert the disaster, or for us to continue to care for our old, sick, helpless, hungry and homeless if it happens."

She was aware that the Catholic Worker movement's longstanding opposition to paying war taxes was an incitement for the IRS to take up such an action. "One of the most costly protests against war, in the long run," Dorothy wrote, "a protest involving enduring personal sacrifice, is to refuse to pay income taxes for war." Dorothy was aware that if the Catholic Worker would file for recognition as a tax-exempt charity, the present demand would be withdrawn, and that many more people would be inclined to make contributions, for they could then deduct the gift from their taxable income. But she could not in conscience apply for any such special recognition. She begged her readers' prayers and understanding. "I'm sure that many will think me a fool indeed, almost criminally negligent, for not taking more care to safeguard . . . the welfare of the lame, halt and blind — deserving and undeserving — that come to us. . . . Our refusal to apply for exemption status in our practice of the works of mercy is part of our protest against war and the present social 'order' which brings wars on today."

News editors recognized an ant-and-elephant story. A report appeared in *The New York Times* under a four-column headline. An editorial in the same paper, titled "Imagination, Please," wondered if the IRS did not have more useful things to do. Many papers took up the story, and supportive letters flooded the Worker's First Street house.

A September date was set for Dorothy to appear in federal court to explain the Catholic Worker's refusal to pay taxes or "structure itself" so as to become tax-exempt. ("We are afraid of that word, 'structure,'" Dorothy wrote in her June column. "We refuse to become a 'corporation.'") She apologized to her readers for the anxiety she felt. "I would like to say . . . that I am not at all worried about this mishmash and the outcome. But of course one becomes intimidated in the awesome presence of a judge, not to speak of stenographers, and swearing to tell the truth, the whole truth, and nothing but the truth, so help me God, and then not being allowed to finish a sentence, or to explain. Anyone who writes as much as I do is not a 'woman of few words!' " She said she had much praying to do, and was finding consolation in reading Tolstoy's *War and Peace.*

"We are not tax evaders," she wrote to readers who thought she was opposed to all taxes. She pointed out that the Catholic Worker quite willingly paid local property taxes, both in New York and Tivoli, and made no attempt to avoid these on religious or charitable grounds.

In July, the IRS withdrew its claim. It was a kind of "absolution," Dorothy wrote with immense relief. She was relieved as well not to have to stand before another judge.

The IRS was no doubt impressed by the support of the press as well as many religious and political figures who had raised their voices on Dorothy's side. By then, she had lived long enough to be seen as prophetic rather than cranky. She had won the respect if not the agreement of a great many people.

On her seventy-fifth birthday in November, the Jesuit magazine *America* did a special issue about her, finding her the individual who best symbolized "the aspiration and action of the American Catholic community during the past forty years." Notre Dame University honored her with its highest award, the Laetare Medal, since she had "comforted the afflicted and afflicted the comfortable virtually all her life." Mother Teresa sent Dorothy a birthday letter from Calcutta: "So much love — so much sacrifice — all for Him alone. You have been such a beautiful branch on the Vine, Jesus, and allowed his Father, the Vine-dresser, to prune you so often and so much. You have accepted all with great love. . . . "

Dorothy was embarrassed by admiration, most of all from those she herself admired. She felt that she was far from being the person she ought to be: less irritable, less judgmental. During Lent in 1973, she wrote to "beg forgiveness" of a former member of the Worker staff, myself, toward whom she felt she had been too harsh. "I want to apologize for my critical attitudes and to promise to amend my life — or attempt to by 'mortifying my critical faculties.' "

A major area of distress for her in the 1970s was what seemed to her the erosion occurring in the spiritual life of her fellow Catholics, including those in the Catholic Worker movement. More than ever Catholics seemed attentive to social issues she had been raising for forty years, but they were increasingly neglectful of the disciplines of Church life that were fundamental to her. "Penance seems ruled out today," she noted repeatedly. It pained her to notice co-workers skipping Mass and not taking the time for prayer: "With prayer, one can go on cheerfully and even happily, while without prayer, how grim is the journey," she commented. "Prayer is as necessary to life as breathing. It is drink and food." She mourned the abandonment by many of the rosary as a tool of prayer and meditation.

She insisted on calling priests "Father" and nuns "Sister" and was annoyed with those who preferred informality. She wished that priests and nuns would retain the traditional clothing which made their vocations visible to strangers. The practice of artificial birth control by Catholics dismayed her, and she was appalled with the growing acceptance of abortion in the larger society: "I say make room for the children. Don't do away with them." She was irked by those who wanted her to say "person" rather than "man": "When I write 'men,' " she commented testily in her column, "I mean 'people.' " She was saddened by the frequent expressions of contempt toward the Pope and bishops—though she granted that there had been popes who reminded her more of vultures than doves. She confessed that she found great pleasure in her tattered, out-of-date English-Latin missals, with "their short, precious accounts of the saints." Her gratitude for Pope John XXIII was undiminished; she regarded him as a saint and published a prayer begging his intercession for the farm workers in one of her columns. But she felt that many were using the renewal he had inspired in order to vandalize the Church. This grieved her, and at times she felt very bitter.

But her sense of duty remained sharp. Despite the quickness with which exhaustion came, she pressed on with travels—in the summer of 1973 going to California, and that winter, in obedience to a request from Mother Teresa, flying to England and Northern Ireland to visit houses of hospitality associated with the Simon Community. Early in 1974 she went to Boston to accept the Isaac Hecker Award from the Paulists. After that she went south by bus, with stops in Washington, Charlottesville, Danville, Atlanta and Tallahassee, among others. From Florida she hurried back to New York in order to speak at Vassar College at Poughkeepsie, not far from the Catholic Worker farm at Tivoli.

But increasingly she had to face her physical limitations. She began to mention "my sick, weak heart" in her columns, and to complain about her failing memory. She had discovered herself answering some letters twice.

She was far from absent-minded about homeless women, who were becoming more numerous in New York. In the March 1974 *Catholic Worker* she described the crowding at the First Street house. "I came back from a short speaking trip to see one woman sleeping on a chair just inside the door, her head on two telephone books resting against a heavy stone statue of St. Joseph which is on the window sill. On still another row of chairs against the wall, another is prone, covered with her coat. Upstairs in the mailing room, there is another young woman, stark upright but with a heavy scarf covering her head and face. If I climb the stairs to the third floor, where seven women with all their belongings fill our limited space, I may find another woman lying against the wall in the hall."

With the financial support of a Trappist community in western New York State, a building for a house just for women was found two blocks away, it was announced in the July 1974 issue. A former music school on East 3rd

Street, it was a large building, three houses that had been joined into one, ideal not only for much expanded hospitality but for the Friday night public meetings. But much work and time was needed — nearly two years, it turned out — before the city issued a certificate of occupancy.

In the meantime, the house on First Street had to meet every need. It seemed to Dorothy more "like a railroad or bus station" than a community. "I'm afraid we are still individualistic, not communitarian." At least "we are getting a lot of work done, and hundreds of meals are put on the table daily." There was also the healing smell of fresh bread baking in the ovens of the Worker kitchen, but even that reminded her at times of all those for whom there was no bread, the millions facing starvation. Dorothy admitted to "a mood of depression."

The Third Stage

Dorothy's first great-grandchild was born in January 1975. It was profoundly comforting news. Announcing it in her column, she began by quoting the Psalm, "Bless the Lord, O my soul, let all that is within me bless His holy name." The same month she went to West Virginia to visit with Catholic Worker families who had gone back to the land. Among them was one of her granddaughters.

Dorothy returned to New York full of encouragement, which she spoke of one night at the Community Church when receiving the Gandhi Award. "They haven't founded 'houses of hospitality on the land,' as some of our farms have been called. Nor are they farming 'communes' or 'agronomic universities,' as other Catholic Worker people have called such ventures. All those high-sounding titles we used to give our little bits of land! These are more like villages, with families living close together, sharing and cooperating in all those many ways that used to be common to any small village. This is happening in the Catholic Worker movement and many other groups working for peace and keeping the nonviolent way. ... There's a strong, strong work going on within the peace movement, with all the joy of youth and the strength of youth, living the normal life of the family — making clothes, raising food, and having babies. So it's a healthy movement, living in the midst of these appalling, murderous times." (Dorothy returned to West Virginia again that year to visit inmates at the Federal Prison for Women at Alderson and to see a nearby Catholic Worker house of hospitality that assisted the inmates' families.)

In the March issue, Dorothy announced her retirement from day-to-day responsibilities. She cited the Buddhist teaching that life was divided into three stages: the first for growing up and basic education, the second for marriage and family and work, and the third for detachment. "The third period is the time for withdrawal from responsibility, letting go of the things of this life, letting God take over." From now on, she said, everything was in the care of "our generous crowd of young people" who put out the paper, take care of the house, and who "perform in truth all the works of mercy."

In the columns that followed, Dorothy stressed prayer more than ever.

In her July column, she recalled a Russian proverb: "In a field where a poisonous weed is found, there is also found the antidote." The times were full of toxic weeds, she said, even though the war in Vietnam was finally over. "For me, the Jesus Prayer, used by the Russian pilgrim, is the remedy growing in the field." It is the simple prayer, "Lord Jesus Christ, Son of God, have mercy on me, a sinner." A classic book of Russian Orthodox spirituality, *The Way of the Pilgrim*, urged its constant use. It is practiced in harmony with each breath.

In September she recommended the prayer Jesus had taught his disciples, the Our Father. "Often I am tempted to depression, thinking that I have scarcely begun the spiritual life, or even to live the life we all profess to, that of voluntary poverty and manual labor. It is a great cleanser of conscience, this living in community, with so many poor and suffering. That harsh saying, 'You love God as much as the one you love the least,' often comes to mind. But just to say over again that one prayer, the Our Father, is to revive, to return to a sense of joy." (Some months later, she wrote with sympathy of a young woman who said to her, "The word 'Father' means nothing to me. It brings me no comfort. I had a drunken father who abused my mother and beat his children." In so many cases, Dorothy commented, "we can do nothing with words. So we are driven to prayer by our helplessness. God takes over.")

She vividly felt her own helplessness. In December she wrote of "the last enemy, death."

In the spring of 1976, following the opening of Maryhouse on East 3rd Street, she felt renewed strength. With Stanley Vishnewski, who had joined the Catholic Worker community in 1934 at the age of seventeen, she drove to Vermont to see her daughter. A pilgrim again, she remembered a song she used for her baby brother John when he was teething: "I'm a pilgrim, I'm a stranger! I can tarry, I can tarry but an hour!"

Dorothy's last speaking trip came a few months later, in August. With Mother Teresa, she had been invited to address the Eucharistic Congress, which that year was meeting in the city of Philadelphia. The date that had been chosen for their speeches was August 6: the feast of the Transfiguration as well as the thirty-first anniversary of the destruction of Hiroshima with the first atom bomb.

For weeks beforehand, Dorothy was in a state of dread about giving the talk. "It is almost easier to stand before a judge than to stand before you," she confessed to an audience of eight thousand when the moment arrived. She had been welcomed with a standing ovation.

Dorothy recalled the events that had led her to the Church and the Eucharist—how the material world "began to speak to my heart of the love of God." The way of the spirit begins with the physical. "It was also the physical aspect of the Church which attracted me"— the bread and wine, the oil and water, the incense.

In the Church she had learned, however, that among the gifts one brings to the altar is our reconciliation with others. "Penance comes before the Eucharist."

"It is a fearful thought," she said after citing the several holocausts of the twentieth century, "that unless we do penance, we will perish. Our Creator gave us life, and the Eucharist to sustain our life. But we have given the world instruments of death of inconceivable magnitude."

It was one of the very rare talks Dorothy had written out beforehand, though she strayed from it often as she stood in the Congress hall. One departure toward the end was an appeal: "Let's all try to be poorer. My mother used to say, 'Everyone take less, and there will be room for one more.' There was always room for one more at our table."

Soon after the Congress, Dorothy went to Pittsburgh for a week-long retreat with Father John Hugo, who once again was being permitted to carry on such work after long years of silence. "I left refreshed and strengthened," Dorothy wrote.

The next month, Dorothy found herself suffering pains in her chest and arms and with a gasping need of fresh air — another heart attack. After electrocardiograms and x-rays at a hospital near the Tivoli farm, she was sent back to her room with orders to rest for at least a month. From her bed, she pondered the Psalm, "Be still and know that I am God."

On the Shelf

"Unto old age and grey hairs, O Lord, forsake me not," Dorothy wrote in *The Catholic Worker's* forty-third anniversary issue in May 1976.

She continued to write "On Pilgrimage" but the pilgrimages now were mainly inner ones. Her news was of prayer, visitors, reading, opera on the radio, plays and films on television, the view from the window, the change of the seasons. She wrote of her struggles with impatience and irritation, her sadness over uprooted trees, and her unhappiness with the anti-piety of some of the young volunteers. She wrote about her memories, mainly from the 1930s. She often recalled her brief travels in Russia.

Often she wrote about death. "When saying the Hail Mary this morning," she wrote in the June 1977 issue, "it suddenly occurred to me how good it is to end our prayer to Mary with 'now and at the hour of our death.' I don't think I had ever realized before how often we pray for the hour of our death, that it would be a good one. It is good, certainly, to have a long period of 'ill health' . . . nothing specific, mild but frightening pains in the heart, and sickness, ebb-tide, the ebbing of life, and then some days of strength and creativity."

She rejoiced that, during her ebb-tide, she was "surrounded by loving kindness. Tulips, a rose, a picture, food. Tender, loving care! We all need it, sick or well."

She gave thanks for the "utterly reliable people" who carried on the active work. The paper was thriving: "We print 94,000 copies, and everyone joins in the job." Maryhouse on East 3rd Street and St. Joseph's on East 1st were carrying on.

Dorothy often wrote about the Jews, remembering various Jewish friends, especially Mike Gold, who had died in 1967. She discovered and repeatedly mentioned the novels of Chaim Potok—*My Name Is Asher Lev*, *The Chosen*, *The Promise*. These were "a joy to read," she said, "full of a sense of the sacramentality of life." She and Potok had memories that nearly touched. "These books are about Brooklyn. Having grown up there, the first seven years, it was intensely interesting to get this picture of the Williamsburg section, where the Hasidic Jews are settled, and to learn about the Hasidim of today, this movement of Jews filled with the fervor and joy of a St. Francis, the men dancing and singing at celebrations." (A few months later, writing about her love of the Bible, she quoted a question from a Potok novel: "I wonder if Gentiles clasp Holy Scripture in their arms and dance with it, as we Jews do?" "Well," she responded, "I've often seen people kiss the Book before and after reading it, and I do myself.")

She recalled various encounters with anti-Semitism in the early years of *The Catholic Worker.* There had been many collisions with the supporters of the notorious (but then much admired) Father Coughlin. "Our papers were torn from our hands and thrown back into our faces, and when I tried to protest, 'But our Lord, Jesus Christ, was a Jew,' the people coming from one meeting shouted at me, 'But He's a long time dead!' "

She remembered an article about anti-Semitism that she had submitted to a prominent Catholic journal. "I was advised," Dorothy wrote, "to stick to my 'delightful, informal essays.' "

Her contemplative eye for the natural world was undiminished. Writing from the beach house on Staten Island for the July 1977 issue, she described the doleful sounds of the mourning dove in one of the nearby mimosa trees. She was enchanted with the mimosa. "No matter how small the seedlings are, they close up their fernlike leaves if you touch them."

Her eyes still took in a great deal, though they tired easily, especially if trying to read small print. Nonetheless, she continued to read a great deal. That month her main book was Pasternak's *Doctor Zhivago,* and she continued with Russian authors month after month. In November she described herself as not so much "housebound" on East 3rd Street as traveling with Chekhov across Siberia to a prison on Sakhalin Island. A few months later, having finished Tolstoy's *Anna Karenina,* she pressed on with his *Resurrection.*

From October 1977 until the following February, she was too weak to leave her room upstairs in Maryhouse. The March issue contained her glad report that she had at last been able to go downstairs and sit in on a Friday night meeting (Bob Gilliam speaking on the Church and tradition). She added that she still lacked "the strength or ambition" to deal with the papers that were piled high on her desk.

Again and again, she was grateful for the volunteers that kept coming to carry on the abrasive, exhausting labor of a house of hospitality, though she noted how few found a vocation in such work. She quoted one of Stanley Vishnewski's funny but accurate comments: "Some come, saying they have found their life work, and remain a few months. Others, more tentative, speak of a visit, and stay."

Her window was a reliable friend, never accusing or demanding, always worth looking through. "Across the street I can see a sycamore tree with a few little seed balls hanging from it. When I first get up and sit by the window, the rising sun at the foot of the street has made it a golden tree, and during the heavy snows, a tree gold and white — a joy to survey."

With the spring of 1978, she was able to come downstairs regularly, for the evening meal and the twice-weekly Mass. But she felt a captive of her frail body. Reporting on the arrest of Robert Ellsberg and Brian Terrell at a nuclear weapons plant in Colorado, she mourned her inability to be present at such actions herself. "I am confined in another way than prison, by weakness and age, but truly I can pray with fervor for those on active duty."

In the summer, she was able to return to Staten Island, but still complained of her sense of confinement. "Patience! Patience!" she wrote in her July column. "The very word patience means *suffering*." She was glad for her years of studying Latin while a student. "Being a journalist, I use many words, and I like to get at the root of them." But patience was harder than etymology. She had wanted to take part in the sit-ins that had just occurred at consulates of the nuclear-weapon states. Among those arrested were twenty members of the Catholic Worker community.

Increasingly she was impatient with her memory. She was haunted by lines of poetry but at times could not recall the authors. " 'Doth it not irk me that upon the beach, the tides monotonous run? Shall I not teach the sea some new speech?' Who wrote it? Those lines came to mind when I woke up this morning." It puzzled her that she should suddenly remember this particular text, as she had no complaint about the speech of the tides. "I love it here."

Among notes about the flowers that were blooming by the back door and her need for two blankets at night if the window was open, she mentioned a visit from Cardinal Cooke "to bring me greetings from Pope Paul! I was overwhelmed by this. How one dreads such honors when inactive. . . . One feels like a figurehead!"

With Tamar and Stanley, she took a walk on the beach collecting beautiful stones. "Every day, I am promising to walk a little more, to get my strength back." But strength evaded her. In the September issue, she wrote that her column would better be named "On the Shelf" rather than "On Pilgrimage." She mentioned how tremulous her handwriting had become. She could no longer write letters.

She mourned Pope Paul's death on Hiroshima Day that August, and was excited to learn that his successor, John Paul I, was the son of a Socialist who had worked in a glass factory. In October she grieved his death, but was pleased with the election of the first non-Italian pope in many centuries, John Paul II from Poland. "I sat at the TV set from the early hours until it was time for our Sunday Mass here at Maryhouse, watching the Inauguration Mass in Rome."

In the fall she wrote about the confusion and irritation she had felt with a prayer book using the term, "Ordinary Time." "To me," she wrote, "no times are 'ordinary.' " (At the time, the Catholic Worker was having one of its more extraordinary times, giving up its farm at Tivoli. "Within a month or two," Deane Mowrer wrote in her monthly column from the farm, "this place will be closed, this community dispersed. I could dwell on the problems, difficulties, defeats, failures, and complain with Ecclesiastes that all is vexation and vanity. I know, however, that most of us in time will remember the joys, friendships, beauty, fulfillment, love, peace, and prayer we have sometimes known here. ... " She pointed out that "the Catholic Worker is not a place, but a way of life.")

In November, on her 81st birthday, Dorothy found that one of the members of the Maryhouse community had put on the wall of her room a huge painting of a pink-robed, orange-haired guardian angel carrying an armload of lilies. "Wildly decorative," Dorothy wrote in her December column. From Tamar she received a beautifully embroidered pillowcase. Among other gifts she especially noted were books by Isaac Bashevis Singer, Dostoyevsky, and a history of Judaism, *Wanderings*, by Chaim Potok. There was a special Mass and afterward a party in the Maryhouse dining room.

While she complained of her memory, much of the time it was reliable and vivid. "I am steeped in memories," she wrote, thinking of the Tivoli farm and the events that had happened there. "I am overcome with nostalgia for the past."

But her eye and thoughts were on the present as well and, as ever, the view from her window. "At exactly 8:05 A.M., the morning sun gilds the upper floors of the buildings across the street, creeping from the grey one to the red brick one. A lovely sight. Pigeons fly from the roofs. Looking up, I see squirrels on the roof edge. The sycamore tree stirs in the cold, east wind. The sky is a cloudless blue. And now one side of the tree, reaching the third floor of those once-luxury tenements, is all gilded, as the sun spreads rapidly around. Young people are on their way to work, but the children are not yet on their way to school. 'My' tree is now radiant with sun!"

Peggy Scherer and other members of the Catholic Worker staff had been visiting in Central America. It was a subject in nearly every issue of the paper, and in Dorothy's thoughts as well. She recalled the committee she had worked for briefly before meeting Peter Maurin. They had sent medical supplies to Sandino's movement in the Nicaraguan mountains and campaigned for the withdrawal of the U.S. Marines. She recalled how John Nevin Sayre, secretary of the Fellowship of Reconciliation, had courageously traveled on mule-back in remote parts of Nicaragua in his efforts to bring about peace in those years. She had been watching Eugene O'Neill's plays on television and remembered the saloon on 6th Avenue where they had spent so many evenings together. Max Bodenheim was one of the others who was often there. She recalled a line of poetry he had recited one night in the saloon's back room: "I know not ugliness, it is a mood which has forsaken me."

She admonished herself to forsake all attachments, to cultivate "holy indifference" — the grateful acceptance of powerlessness. "I should rejoice that I am 'just an old woman,' as the little boy said at dinner in the Rochester House of Hospitality long ago. He said, 'All day long they said Dorothy Day is coming, and now she's here and she's just an old woman!' "

The Mules Are Packed

"My resolution for the new year," Dorothy wrote in the January 1979 *Catholic Worker*, "is to get out and *walk* more." She still felt herself a captive in her room, which at times she compared to a room Dostoyevsky had described in his short story, "The Honest Thief": less a room than a corner. She felt cornered.

Some of those close to her during her last few years sensed that her loneliness deepened with the stripping away of her immense physical strength. She was rarely able to be involved in the decision-making process of the house or even the paper. "But she made of her loneliness monastic solitude," Tom Cornell recalls. She spent at least half an hour in preparation for receiving Communion, which Frank Donovan brought each day from the house chapel, and half an hour in thanksgiving afterward. The rest of the day was punctuated by reading the Psalms and other parts of the monastic office, times of silent prayer, reading, meals, radio and television. There were many for whom she prayed each day, among them various people who had committed suicide. She prayed that those who had taken their own lives would have the grace of final repentance. That her prayers occurred long after the deaths was of no matter, she said. "There is no time with God." The prayers we say now affect an eternal economy.

Tragedy struck in the first weeks of 1979 with the death of her great-grandson, Justin, hit by a car in Vermont. "I feel prostrated," she wrote in her diary. "Grief is numbing."

She wrote of those members of the Worker staff who often experienced death each day through their work at St. Rose's Home, a hospice near the East River for indigent New Yorkers dying of cancer. When she met Peter Maurin, Dorothy remembered, she was reading *Sorrow Built a Bridge*, a biography of Rose Hawthorne Lathrop who founded the order responsible for this hospice and several others.

She recalled how disappointed Peter had been with the first issue of *The Catholic Worker*, which he had hoped would be full of his own essays. "Peter certainly got to the *roots* of our acquisitive society," she went on. His vision had centered on the works of mercy. "But we are so busy with the corporal works of mercy that we often neglect the spiritual ones (converting the sinner, instructing the ignorant, counseling the doubtful, comforting the sorrowful, bearing wrongs patiently, forgiving injuries, and praying for the living and the dead)."

One of the corporal works of mercy was feeding the hungry, but at times Dorothy longed for better cooks to do it. "We had hard baked potatoes for supper, and overcooked cabbage. I'm in favor of becoming a vegetarian only if the vegetables are cooked right." At another meal, she discovered chopped onions, herbs and spices in the fruit salad. "A sacrilege, to treat food this way. Food should be treated with respect, since Our Lord left Himself to us in the guise of food. His disciples knew Him in the breaking of bread." She envied Stanley's ability to eat everything with enthusiasm — a gift he attributed to the fact that he was still a "growing boy."

A few months later she was rejoicing over a fruit salad brought to her by her godchild, Jean Kennedy, though she had a slightly guilty conscience. "I ate it all! How sensual I am. A glutton. Was it St. Catherine of Siena or St. Angela Foligno who wanted to tie a baked chicken around her neck and run through the streets shouting, 'I am a glutton'?"

Her appetite for books remained huge. Among the titles she especially mentioned in 1979 and 1980 were Solzhenitsyn's *The First Circle*, Tolstoy's *War and Peace*, *The Third Man* by Graham Greene, *All the King's Men* by Robert Penn Warren, and two classics of the spiritual life, *The Little Flowers of St. Francis* and *The Imitation of Christ*. Dostoyevsky remained indispensable; she reread *The Idiot*, *The Possessed*, and *Crime and Punishment*. Increasingly, however, she turned to television. Among films she watched were *Wuthering Heights*, *Gone with the Wind*, and *The African Queen*. Radio and television broadcasts of opera were a particular joy, though hardly a new one. Wagner was her favorite composer. She recalled that, many years earlier, a couple associated with the Catholic Worker farm at Easton had been scandalized to discover that Dorothy had been to the Metropolitan Opera House for Richard Strauss' *Salome*.

On Easter 1979, Cesar Chavez came to visit her. In June Mother Teresa came to Maryhouse and had her last visit with Dorothy.

That summer and the next, her condition prevented a stay at the beach house on Staten Island.

In her July 1979 column, she shared with readers a letter from her sister-in-law, Tina de Aragon Feldman, who had just learned that she was suffering from cancer of the spinal cord. "I was given the verdict at St. Vincent's Hospital. For two hours, I was in mortal terror. Then, a thought came to me. Not an experience, just a thought out of St. Teresa's writings about her wanderings along the roads of Spain. 'The mules are packed, they are kicking, the road will be rocky, but the destination is sure.' St. Teresa encourages familiarity with God. This descendant of converts, very female, very stormy, very valiant, does not want us to fall back from the quest in awe of greatness. She asks that we join her in all our failing humanity, since there is nothing to disturb or afright us except, perhaps, vermin in uncomfortable inns."

Dorothy felt that her own mules were packed. "The paper is in the hands of young people," she said to Robert Ellsberg during a visit, "and the houses are strong. My prayer is, 'Now let thy servant depart in peace.'"

In November, Stanley Vishnewski died. "It must have been the soup," he said with a smile to those at his bedside. He had been forty-five years with the Catholic Worker, though he still reminded staff and visitors that he hadn't yet decided whether or not to stay. He was a man of great spiritual depth and, at the same time, the court jester of the Catholic Worker — which he often called the Catholic Shirker movement. "The Catholic Worker is made up of saints and martyrs," he was famous for saying. "You have to be a martyr to put up with the saints." He had become the Worker's resident historian, but his book about the movement's early years, *Wings of the Dawn*, hadn't found a publisher when he died. "I can truthfully say," he told his co-workers, "that I have been rejected by some of the best publishers in America." (This wonderfully lively book was published in 1985 by the Catholic Worker, which sells it, Catholic Worker fashion, for whatever the buyer offers, from nothing on up. Stanley would approve. "Here we practice the economics of the Kingdom of Heaven. Everything is free. It is also already broken in. I have a suit that was test-worn for eight years before I agreed to accept delivery.")

There was no "On Pilgrimage" that month, but in December Dorothy wrote his obituary, "A Knight for a Day," the last article of her life (though her column continued, with entries from her diary). She remembered Stanley's arrival as a seventeen-year-old Lithuanian from Brooklyn, and how in the early years he had once rescued her when she was pinned against a wall by a police horse being used against a picket line, and how in later years he rescued her from a demented veteran who nearly crushed her at the Tivoli farm. "Stanley used to come, these recent years," Dorothy wrote, "and have dinner with me, and we watched television."

"On Pilgrimage" was again missing in the January 1980 issue, but in February a series of one and two sentence diary notes appeared. She was enjoying Dorothy Sayers' *Gaudy Night*, had heard Wagner's *Siegfried* on the radio, and seen *How Green Was My Valley* on television. She noted that Deane Mowrer and others from the Worker community in New York were off to Washington for a week-long vigil at the Pentagon. There was but the hint of frustration at her being unable to go along: "It would be ungrateful," the column ended, "not to find enjoyment in my inactivity, not to 'rejoice always,' as the psalmist says. Was it Ruskin who wrote about 'the duty of delight'? What a nice phrase!"

In her diary for March, she recalled the saying so often repeated in *The Catholic Worker*: "The less you have of Caesar's, the less you have to render to Caesar." She had heard Wagner's *Parsifal* on the radio.

In April, her sister, Della, died. They had been close throughout their lives, constant friends to one another, and in earlier years her death would have brought forth a long essay in the paper. Now Dorothy wrote simply: "My most dear sister Della died yesterday."

On May 1, noting in her diary that it was *The Catholic Worker*'s forty-seventh anniversary, she recalled the distribution of the first issue on Union Square, mentioned the special Mass and dinner at Maryhouse, and then added, "How one misses a sister!"

She was reading Dorothy Sayers' *Five Red Herrings* and had heard more Wagner on the radio.

In June she wrote in her diary that she was too weak to receive visitors. She was praying, watching television, and listening to the radio.

In her July diary, she noted Ammon Hennacy's birthday on the 24th. "He would have been eighty-seven years old today." She was rereading Mike Gold's novel, *Jews Without Money*.

In August, on the feast of St. Augustine, she copied down her favorite passage from Augustine's *Confessions*: "What is it that I love when I love my God? It is a certain light that I love and melody and fragrance and embrace that I love when I love my God — a light, melody, fragrance, food, embrace of the God-within, where, for my soul, that shines which space does not contain; that sounds which time does not sweep away; that is fragrant which the breeze does not dispel; and that tastes sweet which, fed upon, is not diminished; and that clings close which no satiety disparts — this is what I love when I love my God."

Dorothy's last "On Pilgrimage" appeared in the October *Catholic Worker*. It began with praise for televised Masses — "wonderful for shut-ins." She was watchful of signs of life outside her window: "The morning glories are up to the third floor of Maryhouse. I can see them grow each day!" She was reading Dorothy Sayers' short stories about Lord Peter Wimsey. She mentioned watching Kenneth Clarke's "Civilisation" series on television, which reminded her of something that Peter Maurin had said: "The thirteenth, the greatest of centuries." Once again, she wrote about Eugene O'Neill and Mike Gold. "I still have a beautiful postcard from Mike when he was visiting Russia when the Catholic Worker was still on Chrystie Street." She was looking forward to watching a play based on Dostoyevsky's *Crime and Punishment.* She had been able to walk a little in the hall one day, "getting my 'sea-legs' under me." After all, she noted, she was a descendant of seagoing people — whalers. She was grateful to Fr. Lyle Young, one of the priests most involved with the Catholic Worker household, for the copies of *The New Yorker* he passed on to her. She recalled something her sister Della used to say: "Had I foreseen what was to befall me, I would have rued the day." She missed traveling, especially by bus. "You feel you are really seeing the country, as you speed along the highway, over plain and mountain."

Her final words in the column were about the "beautiful statue of the Madonna behind the altar in the Maryhouse chapel, which Tina de Aragon, my sister-in-law, carved for us from *lignum vitae*."

On November 29, on the eve of the First Sunday of Advent, Dorothy talked with Eileen Egan on the telephone. She had been watching a news report about the survivors of an earthquake in southern Italy who were struggling to keep themselves alive in mountain snows. "Her voice was strong with compassion," Eileen recalls. "She asked me what was being done for them by Catholic Relief Services, and was relieved to hear about the emergency air shipment of blankets, food and medicine. Dorothy suggested that the blankets could also be made to serve as tents."

Later in the afternoon, Tamar came to visit. During the visit, Dorothy asked for a cup of tea and remarked how good life can be at certain moments. She held Tamar's hand. At 5:30 P.M., Dorothy's tired heart stopped. It was a death as quiet as the turning of a page.

Deo Gratias

Dorothy's body, dressed in a blue-and-white-check dress, was placed in a plain, unvarnished pine coffin that was set on top of the altar in the chapel at Maryhouse. The coffin was adorned with a single long-stemmed rose. A prie-dieu was placed in front of it, its red plush worn thin by years of kneeling. Above the coffin was a cross made of two pieces of driftwood, such as Dorothy had often collected on the beach at Staten Island. Tina de Aragon's Madonna stood close by.

"Dorothy looked so thin, so old and fragile and shrunken," Tom Cornell wrote a few days later, "but still beautiful and strong. Her cheekbones and her chin and her mouth were as ever, and there was a look of peace in her face."

The day following her death and long into the night, visitors came to the wake to pay their respects and share their memories. Many knelt in prayer before the coffin, at times praying in tears. Some kissed her forehead or touched her face lightly. In death as in life, Dorothy was surrounded by unlikely friends and companions, ranging from those "living rough" on the streets to well-known writers, editors and teachers. Some were distinguished in the Christian community, while others were distinguished for their troubles in that same community. The Christians predominated but they could not claim a monopoly on Dorothy. There was a wide variety of believers, but some atheists too, and some who were a bit of both. There were those who either had no unusual political convictions or were convinced of views far to the right (or left) of Dorothy. Some were there simply because they had found in the Catholic Worker a channel through which money given away actually reached the poor.

In a room adjacent to the chapel, many stories were told over coffee. There were moments of laughter, and others of silence.

In the morning, Dorothy's grandchildren carried the coffin to the Nativity Mission Church, half a block away, the parish in which Dorothy and others in the Catholic Worker community had often shared in the Mass. At the entrance to the church, Cardinal Cooke blessed Dorothy's body. A huge crowd had turned out, as diverse a mixture as could be found in any New York City subway car. Some had traveled thousands of miles. Among the mourners was Forster Batterham, whom Dorothy had always referred to as her husband, even after a half-century's separation.

There were many reporters. One of them asked Peggy Scherer, editor of *The Catholic Worker*, whether the movement could continue without its founder. "We have lost Dorothy," Peggy replied, "but we still have the gospel."

Dorothy was buried in a donated grave at Resurrection Cemetery on Staten Island, a grassy meadow overlooking the ocean within walking distance of the beach house where Dorothy's conversion had occurred.

A small stone was set over the grave, ornamented with a loaves-and-fishes design by Ade Bethune that had often been used in *The Catholic Worker*. The stone's text was brief:

DOROTHY DAY

NOVEMBER 8, 1897–NOVEMBER 29, 1980

DEO GRATIAS

A Personal Remembrance

I first met Dorothy a few days before Christmas in 1960. On leave from my job with the U.S. Navy in Washington, I had come to New York to visit the Catholic Worker after reading copies of the newspaper that I found in my parish library. My first few days were spent at Saint Joseph's House (then on Spring Street in the midst of an Italian neighborhood, but soon to move a few blocks away to a building on Chrystie Street). From there I went to the Catholic Worker's rural outpost on the southern tip of Staten Island. In the large, faded dining room of an old farmhouse, I found half a dozen people gathered around a pot of tea and a pile of mail at one end of a large table. Dorothy Day was reading leading letters aloud.

What a handsome woman! Her face was long, with high, prominent cheekbones underlining large, quick eyes that could be teasing one moment and laughing the next. Her hair was braided and circled the top of her head like a garland of silver flowers. The suit she wore was plain and well-tailored, good quality and yet almost certainly from the Catholic Worker clothing room on Spring Street, a distribution center for discarded garments open daily, except Sundays, to street people.

The only letter I still recall from that day's reading was one from Thomas Merton, the famous monk whose autobiography, *The Seven Storey Mountain*, had held many people in its grip, including me. Nineteen years earlier, Merton had withdrawn from "the world" to a Trappist monastery with a slam of the door that eventually was heard around the world. I had assumed he wrote to no one outside his family. Yet here he was in correspondence with someone who was not only in the thick of the world, but one of its more controversial figures.

In his letter, Merton told Dorothy that he was deeply touched by her witness for peace, which had several times resulted in arrest and imprisonment. "You are right in going along the lines of *satyagraha* [Gandhi's term for nonviolent action; literally the power of truth]. I see no other way. ... Nowadays it is no longer a question of who is right but who is at least not criminal. ... It has never been more true than now that the world is lost in its own falsity and cannot see true values. ... God bless you." This was one of Merton's first letters to Dorothy. Before long he was publishing

147

articles in *The Catholic Worker*, and getting into trouble within his religious order for doing so.

Merton was one of countless people drawn to Dorothy and influenced by her. She had a great gift for making those who met her, even if only through letters or her published writings, look at themselves in a new light and question their ideas, allegiances, and choices.

I met her when I was 19 and she was 63. Half a year later, after being discharged from the Navy as a conscientious objector, I joined the Catholic Worker staff in New York.

While writing this book, I read an account by Jack English of Dorothy as she was twenty-five years before I met her. Jack had missed the talk Dorothy had given at his college, but the next day he found discussion about her raging in the cafeteria. "They were talking about how beautiful she was. She had talked the entire lecture with a cigarette hanging out of the corner of her mouth, with a beret on, and someone said it looked as if she needed her neck washed." Jack was so intrigued that he decided to attend a meeting Dorothy was addressing that night in a nearby town. He found her amazing. "What impressed me so much was that she said, 'You can do this work *wherever* you are.'" Afterward Dorothy and Jack talked briefly. She urged him to read *The Catholic Worker*. "That was the beginning of it. Something happened in my life. It wasn't a profound thing at the moment. She was not the kind of person that had been described to me that morning in the coffee room. I had read some of the lives of holy people and saints, but I had the feeling of the same dedication and even I hate to use the word *holiness* about Dorothy."

Recalling his first impressions about Dorothy in a taped interview with Deane Mowrer in 1970, Jack said he was still impressed with Dorothy's ability to engage herself with so many individuals. "She occasionally talks in terms of the abstract, but she never talks or operates except person to person." Jack had learned from her that "each human being is unique, totally unique, and that each time I meet and have a real encounter with another human being, I am changed somehow, whether for good or bad."

The Dorothy Day I met was a quarter century older than the one Jack had met in the mid-1930s. Both the cigarette and beret were long gone. Dorothy had become even more formidable and was on the edge of being venerable. But the main qualities that so impressed Jack were just as striking to me: her ability to focus on the person she was talking to, not to see just a young face but *your* face, not discerning just a vague, general promise, but *your* particular gifts. Through Dorothy, you saw exciting possibilities in yourself you hadn't seen before. Also you saw what it meant to lead a life that was relentlessly God-centered. She blew the idea of saints as sugar-coated people out the window.

Her impact on Jack was similar to her impact on me. We both became involved in Catholic Worker houses of hospitality, which were found then, as now, in many cities.

Catholic Worker houses, while always having unique aspects, still have a lot in common. They are unpretentious places in run-down neighborhoods where down-and-out people are received and necessities given, all without forms, inquisitors, or unsought advice. Perhaps there is some angel in heaven who knows exactly how many bowls of soup have been served in Catholic Worker houses since 1933. Millions, that's certain. Jack and I have both served our share of them, along with thousands of others who have been part of Catholic Worker communities down through the years. The remarkable thing about Catholic Worker soup is that it has a way of making you ask questions—Dorothy Day's questions—about what brings about a social order in which so many people are defeated and have to line up at the doors of soup kitchens.

Being part of the Catholic Worker household in New York City was a mixed blessing. At that time, probably it was one of the less happy communities in the Catholic Worker movement. In fact we were hardly a community at all. But there was one great blessing about being in that stressful setting; it was getting to know Dorothy, and to be known by her.

As I had discovered that first day at the farm on Staten Island, she was a wonderful and tireless story teller. She didn't just read the letters she received to herself, but read them aloud to those she worked with, oftentimes telling about the people who sent them.

I recall her reading a letter from the Gauchat family, founders of a Catholic Worker community in Ohio. Dorothy told us how the Gauchats had taken in a six-month-old child who was expected to die at any time. The child was deaf and blind, with a fluid-filled lump on his head larger than a baseball. "Bill Gauchat made the sign of the cross over that child's face," Dorothy said, "and he saw those dull eyes followed the motion of his hand. The child *could* see! Within a year David—that was his name— was well enough to be taken home by his real parents. His life was saved by the love in the Gauchat home."

Hearing stories like these day after day, we were learning something about life that you don't get in any classroom or even in many churches. At the core of each story there were always just a few people, maybe just one person, for whom following Christ was the most important thing in the world. What astonishing things came from that kind of discipleship!

Another story I recall her telling had to do with a prostitute named Mary Ann with whom Dorothy was briefly in prison in Chicago in the early 1920s. Dorothy hadn't planned to be arrested and was terrified of the guards. "You must hold your head high," Mary Ann told her, "and give them no clue that you're afraid of them or ready to beg for anything, any favors whatsoever. But you must see them for what they are—never forget that they're in jail too."

Some stories you would hear more than once from Dorothy if you remained near her long enough. Some sayings you were bound to hear frequently, even if you were only there for a short time. How many times have I heard her repeat St. Catherine of Siena's remark, "All the way to heaven is heaven, because Jesus said, 'I am the way.'" There was a line from George Bernanos that she often used: "Hell is not to love anymore." Everyone at the Catholic Worker knew Dostoyevsky had said, "The world will be saved by beauty." And there were *many* others.

Recalling how often she quoted others, it is only fair to note that Dorothy was very much a borrower of other people's ideas and entirely unembarrassed about doing so. Her words tended to be as second-hand as her clothing, though the connections she made and the passion with which she spoke was all her own. Apart from the Bible, her main sources were the saints plus a few novelists whose books were basically religious. Among the saints, those she most often cited were Paul, Benedict, Francis, Catherine of Siena, Teresa of Avila, John of the Cross, and Therese of Lisieux.

Dorothy had much in common with Saint Teresa of Avila. Both had animated the foundation of many religious communities, and both were tireless travelers until old age made it impossible to travel further. Both were reformers who went through periods of being regarded as possible heretics. Both were outspoken and fearless.

But another Theresa, Therese of Lisieux, "the Little Flower," also inspired her. The only biography Dorothy ever wrote was about Therese and her Little Way. "The significance of our smallest act!" Dorothy said in that book. "The significance of the little things we leave undone! The protests we do not make, the stands we do not take, we who are living in the world!" (Extensive excerpts from Therese are included in *Dorothy Day: Selected Writings*.)

Again and again in her writing and talks, Dorothy would stress the "little way." It was at the heart of everything she valued: "Paper work, cleaning the house, dealing with the innumerable visitors who come all through the day, answering the phone, keeping patience and acting intelligently, which is to find some meaning in all that happens—these things, too, are the works of peace, and often seem like a very little way."

Dorothy had been, since childhood, a great reader. Her engagement in the world seemed only to fuel this side of her life. Certain books she read over and over again—I think of Dickens's *Bleak House* and Dostoyevsky's *The Brothers Karamazov*. One can wonder whether the figure of Father Zossima in *The Brothers Karamazov* isn't a co-founder of the Catholic Worker, so much did Dorothy value the old monk's teaching on active love. (The monk in the novel was partly inspired by Father Amvrosy of Optina Pustin, to whom Dostoyevsky turned in a time of personal tragedy. When I took part in the canonization of Father Amvrosy at a monastery near Moscow in 1988, I thought that surely Dorothy was among the saints invisibly present to celebrate the day with me.)

In this period of acute nervousness about sexual roles, there is some hesitancy to say anyone is or ever was feminine, but Dorothy certainly was that. As she was usually ill at ease when anyone pointed a camera at her,

her femininity rarely shows in her photos. Hers was a hearty femininity, such as you find in Chaucer's Wife of Bath. Like the Wife of Bath, she could be, indeed often was, shocking in her plain-speaking way. She was able to tell a bawdy joke, much to the dismay of some of those who happened to encounter this side of Dorothy. She was also, at times, surprisingly shy, almost girlish, long after she had acquired grey hair. Then again, she could be as fierce and determined as one of those Russian women who repaired the streets and kept going to church even in the years of Stalin.

Her direct, at times shocking, way of getting to the heart of things was much in evidence one night when she was speaking to a Catholic student group at New York University, not far from Washington Square Park. The Cold War was at its most frozen in that packed and smokey room. Clearly some of those present considered Dorothy an acolyte of the Kremlin. One of them demanded to know what Dorothy would do if the Russians invaded the United States. Would she not admit that in this extreme, at least, killing was justified, even a duty? "We are taught by Our Lord to love our enemies," Dorothy responded without batting an eye. "I hope I could open my heart to them with love, the same as anyone else. We are all children of the same Father." There was a brief but profound quiet in the room before Dorothy went on to speak about nonviolent resistance and efforts to convert opponents.

Probably nothing made Dorothy more nervous than adulation. Some people looked at her as if they could actually see a bright halo floating over her head. I don't know how often Dorothy made that famous remark— "Don't call me a saint; I don't want to be dismissed so easily." Maybe only once. But anyone who knew her was aware of how she would escape from those who treated her as a walking holy relic. Joe Zarella tells the story of someone approaching Dorothy and asking, "Miss Day, do you have visions?" Dorothy's response, according to Joe, was, "Oh, shit!" (These are the kind of stories you find in Rosalie Riegle Troester's superb oral history, *Voices from the Catholic Worker.*)

As I have come to realize while writing this book, Dorothy's embarrassment and annoyance in the face of a certain kind of admiration was not only genuine modesty. Rather she felt that many of these people would view her quite differently if they knew her better—knew her faults, and knew more about her past. She felt she had helped create an idealized image of herself by leaving out of her two autobiographies events she found particularly shameful in the years preceding her entrance into the Catholic Church, her abortion most of all.

It was clear in the New York Catholic Worker community that Dorothy didn't want any of us to read the one thing she had written about the abortion and the sad affair it was rooted in, her novel, *The Eleventh Virgin*. As far as I am aware, we all respected her wish without even knowing why she disliked the book so intensely. Not that the book would have been easily found in any event.

She once told her friend Bob Coles (the psychiatrist best known for his books on children in crisis) about the effort she had made earlier in her life to find and destroy every copy of the novel. Finally Dorothy brought this book-burning effort of hers to the attention of her confessor. The priest laughed. "My, my," he said. "I thought he was going to tell me to stop being so silly and mixed up in my priorities," Dorothy said to Coles. "I will remember to my last day here on God's earth what the priest said: 'You can't have much faith in God if you're taking the life he has given you and using it that way.' I didn't say a word in reply. The priest added, 'God is the one who forgives us, if we ask Him; but it sounds like you don't even want forgiveness—just to get rid of the books.'" (The story comes from Robert Coles's book, *Dorothy Day: A Radical Devotion*, which is mainly made up of Coles's remarkable conversations with Dorothy over a period of years.) Little by little, those closest to her became aware of the sins of her more hidden past and perhaps helped her to carry some of the pain of it.

To return to photos of Dorothy, you might get the idea looking at them that she had rather a bleak personality. While she was often a person of the utmost seriousness, those who never met her can't begin to understand the impact Dorothy had on others unless they can imagine how easy it was to be with her, how welcome one felt in her company. Much of her time was spent sitting at the table where meals were served, just sipping tea or coffee and talking to whoever joined her, sometimes speaking in an aminated way, sometimes mainly listening.

When Dorothy was present, she was completely present. But often she wasn't there at all. She was either visiting other Catholic Worker houses and speaking at churches and colleges, or staying at the Catholic Worker farm or at the beach house on Staten Island. In the New York house, being as centered on Dorothy as it was during the time I was part of it, her periods away left a hole that no one else could fill. She had delegated various responsibilities: handling the household money, having charge of the kitchen, managing the paper (though she was definitely the editor and publisher), taking care of the address list, and running the farm. But no one was in a position to make a decision in her absence which everyone else would accept. In the New York house, she alone could lay down the law, which at times was urgently needed.

During the period I was part of Saint Joseph's House in New York, 1961-62, we went through a number of nasty battles during times when Dorothy was away. Perhaps the worst was brought on by a decision made by the two-person kitchen crew to give the occasional pound of butter or box of eggs that was contributed to those coming on "the line"—the generally anonymous people who turned up for meals—rather than to "the family," the much smaller group of people who had become regulars, were known by name, were living at the Catholic Worker, and had a job to do within the household. The family ate after the line. The family, who had seen many volunteers come and go, were outraged, and the staff itself—six or eight people at the time—bitterly divided. It was in the aftermath of "the great butter crisis," late in 1961, that Dorothy appointed me as managing editor of the paper. I had just turned 20.

Conflicting quotations from Dorothy's writings began to appear on the community bulletin board, each faction hurling explosive bits of Dorothy at the other. On the one hand there would be a quotation from Dorothy declaring that we must be ready to roll up in old newspapers, giving our beds to those who needed them; and on the other hand a text in which Dorothy reflected that we must accept our limitations; that this too was voluntary poverty.

After some days Dorothy was back again. Without bothering to reconcile the quotations, she said (with the finality of a monastery's abbot) that the butter and eggs were to go, as before, to the family. The result was, in the end, that the two people resigned, convinced that Dorothy Day was a fraud. In brief, she hadn't lived up to her own quotations.

These events, while petty and even comic when viewed from the outside, were grueling from the inside. There must have been hundreds of blow-ups as bad or worse during the forty-seven years that lay between the founding of the Catholic Worker and Dorothy's death. It is an endless cause of wonder to me that, despite all these harsh trials within the community, she nonetheless retained her capacity for faith, hope, and love down to the last day of her life. (A phrase she often used was "the duty of hope.")

For my part, one of the things I learned at the Catholic Worker (which Dorothy often defined as a school) was that the poverty-stricken for whom the houses of hospitality existed were often easier to live with and more merciful than the young volunteers who knew more about ideology than defeat in life. Yet for all our shortcomings, we did manage to get a great deal done: Food begged and bought, meals cooked and served, clothes received and given away, dishes washed, floors scrubbed, sheets laundered, bread baked, the paper mailed out, the mailing list kept up-to-date, people with medical needs assisted, and hand-written thank-you notes sent out to each and every donor, no matter how small the gift—all that and much more.

Not the smallest problem in the house was the noise. I recall one day trying to carry on a conversation with Dorothy about an article we were thinking about using in the next issue. We were at her desk in a tiny office next to the front door of the house on Chrystie Street, just in front of the area in which meals were served. It was the noisiest floor in the house. That morning we could hardly hear each other. In the middle of a sentence, Dorothy got out of her chair, opened the door, and then yelled loud enough for a corpse to blink, "Holy silence!" Silence, such as a Trappist monk might envy, briefly reigned at Saint Joseph's House.

Dorothy's ability to survive community life and even to see good in those of us who came to help was surely due to the depth and intensity of her spiritual life. It was obvious to anyone who was in sight of Dorothy for more than a few hours that she was a woman of prayer.

When I think of her, I recall her first of all on her knees. This might be at the nearest parish church or the chapel at the Catholic Worker farm. (The archdiocese had permitted a chapel on the farm and reservation of the sacrament within it.) Dorothy would spend a good deal of time every day on her knees, praying. I looked in the prayer books she left on the bench one day and discovered page after page of names, all written in her careful italic script, of people, living and dead, for whom she was praying. She prayed as if lives depended on it. "We feed the hungry, yes," she said. "We try to shelter the homeless and give them clothes, but there is strong faith at work; we pray. If an outsider who comes to visit us doesn't pay attention to our praying and what that means, then he'll miss the whole point."

She went to Mass every day until her body wasn't up to it and even then still received Communion every day, carefully preparing before and giving plenty of time afterward for thanksgiving. She went to confession at least once a week. She loved the rosary and prayed it often. "If we love enough," she once noted, "we are importunate: we repeat our love as we repeat Hail Marys on the rosary." She also used the Jesus Prayer and recommended its use to others.

It was striking to me how deep was her love for Christians of other churches, but especially for the Orthodox churches. What was at the root of her special affinity to Orthodoxy, I don't know. Perhaps it had to do with her Russian friendships, and the special place Dostoyevsky had played in the formation of her vocation. The first time I visited an Orthodox church it was with Dorothy, and the first time I attended the magnificent Orthodox Liturgy it was with her as well. In the early 1960s, she was a friend of a priest serving at the Russian Orthodox Cathedral on East 97th Street in Manhattan, Father Matthew Stadniuk from Moscow, who became an occasional visitor both to Saint Joseph's House and the farm. (Back in Moscow in later years, he was the priest who first got his parishioners into voluntary service at a local hospital when, in the new climate that flourished under Gorbachev, religious believers were no longer excluded from a social role.)

Dorothy's longing for the repair of the rift dividing eastern and western Christianity drew her into the Third Hour group, perhaps the only place in Manhattan at the time where people met who had in common a love of Orthodoxy, whether or not they were Orthodox themselves. I can remember sitting next to her at a Third Hour meetings, trying to make sense of the Russian words she and others used so comfortably.

Her commitment to the Catholic Church was never at issue. In fact it disturbed many people, including some in the Catholic Worker community, that she was such a devout Catholic, so wholehearted in her acceptance of Catholic teaching and the church's hierarchical structure. She was critical not of what the church taught but rather its failure to live out its teaching.

Dorothy found Catholicism the Christian body least trapped in nationalism. Perhaps still more important to her, it was the church most crowded with the poor. Also it was the dispenser of sacraments without which life was, for her, barren.

Dorothy often stressed obedience (the root meaning of which is "listening"), insisting that if she were ordered to stop publishing *The Catholic Worker*, she would do so, though not without trying first to change the cardinal's mind. "You mean," I asked her one day, "if the cardinal says we have to give up our stand on war, we give it up?" "Not at all," she said. "But then we might only use quotations from the Bible, the sayings of the saints, extracts from papal encyclicals, just nothing of our own." She said that if there was no alternative but to stop publishing the paper, she would do so, hoping others might carry on. Then she quoted the Gospel: "Unless the seed fall into the ground and die, it cannot bring forth new life."

Her devotion to the church, however, was not without critical bite. She often spoke of the church as being "the cross on which Christ was crucified." Though the metaphor sounds poetic, it was no compliment. Similarly Dorothy occasionally remarked that the net Peter had lowered into the human sea once Jesus made him a fisher of men "caught many blowfish and quite a few sharks." There were priests and bishops who reminded her "far more of Cain than of Abel."

However striking an individual Dorothy might seem, her ideas were not individualistic. Part of the value of the church for her was that it brought people together across many lines of division—political, ideological, economic, geographic, even the borders drawn by time, as she often remarked that "there is no time with God." Her early attraction to radical movements probably had a similar impetus: people coming together in a spirit of self-sacrifice to make the world a more caring place in which no one is thrown into the garbage heap. She often pointed out that it wasn't the church that led her to the poor, but radicals. It was the radicals who were asking why there were so many hungry, homeless, jobless people in a world that has the means to meet everyone's needs.

The friendships that she formed with a number of radicals she maintained quite openly right through the Cold War to the end of her life, never letting ideological differences or political expediency get the upper hand. When Elizabeth Gurley Flynn—one of America's leading Communists—died, she left her small estate of clothing, books and furniture to Saint Joseph's House.

Dorothy's commitment to people who somehow became part of her extended family was one of her most striking traits. She might at certain moments be quite harsh in what she had to say when a matter of principle was at stake, yet I can testify from my own experience that not only did she never end a relationship because of disagreement, but she would sooner or later beg forgiveness, sometimes in the most abject way.

I noted earlier that, in ideas, Dorothy was a great borrower. But her way of seeing things was very much her own. I think, for example, of what happened one day when a co-worker and I were clearing out rubbish from a small apartment one flight up in a cold-water tenement on Ridge Street. Dorothy was having increasing trouble managing the five flights to the apartment she had been living in on Spring Street. These two rooms could be reached more easily. Stuart and I dragged box after box of debris down to the street, including a hideous (so it seemed to us) painting on plywood of the Holy Family. Mary, Joseph, and Jesus had been painted in a few bright colors against a battleship grey background. We shook our heads, deposited it in the trash along the curb, and went back to continue cleaning. Not long after, Dorothy arrived, the plywood painting in hand. "Look what I found! The Holy Family! It's a providential sign, a blessing." She put it on the mantle of the apartment's extinct fireplace. I looked at it again and this time saw it was a work of love and faith, however simply rendered. If it was no Renaissance masterpiece, it had its own beauty. But I wouldn't have thought so if Dorothy hadn't seen it first.

Dorothy is no longer with us. At least we can't sit down and have a cup of tea with her anymore. But there is no doubt that she remains a vital presence. Many regard her as a saint, and not as a way of keeping her at a safe distance. There are historians who describe her as the most influential American Catholic of the last hundred years. Perhaps it is true. In any event, she set an example which continues to influence many people. One can say she helped bring about a reformation that centered on the Catholic Church but reached far beyond it. It is not a reformation emphasizing theological doctrine but one rooted in the sacredness of life, the truth that we are each made in the image and likeness of God, and the real presence of Christ in the poor. She gave an example of hospitality and mercy as a way of life. "We are here to *celebrate* Him," she declared, "through works of mercy."

To put it as simply as possible, she gave an example of active love. "Love is the measure," she so often said, "by which we will be judged."

Jim Forest
Feast of St. Teresa of Avila, 1993

Sources

Dorothy Day has left us quite a lot of writing. The most enduring self-portrait was *The Long Loneliness*. Yet one finds a cautionary note about the book among Dorothy Day's papers in the Catholic Worker Archive at Marquette University in Milwaukee.: "It is always called my autobiography but it is really a selection of periods of my life searching for God and not a story giving the whole truth. . . . I feel, to put it simply, that it is not the truth about me . . . [but] only part of the truth."

From Union Square to Rome (Preservation of the Faith Press, 1939) was still less candid about events Dorothy preferred not to recall. It was only in her novel, *The Eleventh Virgin* (Albert & Charles Boni, 1924), that she describes her abortion and her love affair with the unborn child's father; in the novel she slightly alters names but otherwise it seems a work of autobiography.

The Long Loneliness has been the major source for my own biography of Dorothy, and is the book most often quoted in the chapters referring to her first half century, though at specific points (indicated in the text) I have relied on *The Eleventh Virgin*.

The other major source I have made extensive use of is Dorothy's column, which appeared nearly every month for much of her life. Some of the columns were collected into books: *House of Hospitality* (Sheed & Ward, 1939), *On Pilgrimage* (Catholic Worker Books, 1948), and *On Pilgrimage: The Sixties* (Curtis Books, 1972). The last has been the major source used for those chapters which concern events of the 1960s.

In writing this book I was also greatly helped by Robert Ellsberg's collection of Dorothy's writings, published by Alfred A. Knopf as *By Little and By Little* and now available from Orbis Books as *Dorothy Day: Selected Writings*. An earlier anthology, *A Penny a Copy: Readings from The Catholic Worker*, edited by Tom Cornell and myself and published by Macmillan in 1968, was also a useful source. (A new, updated edition of this book is to be issued by Orbis in 1994.)

Other help came from William R. Miller's books, *A Harsh and Dreadful Love: Dorothy Day and the Catholic Worker Movement* (Liverwright, 1973) and *Dorothy Day: A Biography* (Harper & Row, 1982).

Deane Mowrer has recorded many interviews with persons associated with the Catholic Worker movement. These have been transcribed and are among the Catholic Worker Papers at Marquette. They provide helpful background reading in better understanding the earlier years of the Catholic Worker. The remembrance of Dorothy Day by Jack English is from one of the Mowrer interviews.

Eileen Egan's essays, especially "Dorothy Day and the Permanent Revolution" (Benet Press, 1984), were a helpful source for chapters touching on Dorothy's travels in Europe and Asia.

For details of the FBI file on the Catholic Worker, see Robert Ellsberg's article, "An Unusual History from the FBI" (*The Catholic Worker*, May and June 1979).

Quotations from speeches by Dorothy Day in the 1970s come from tape recordings in my possession.

I have drawn on many stories and memories that either were my own or have been shared with me by friends, especially Tom and Monica Cornell and Robert Ellsberg.

Further Reading

The Long Loneliness is not only Dorothy's best and most popular book but is likely to become a classic of religious autobiography. First issued in 1952 by Harper & Row, it remains in print with HarperSanFrancisco. Dorothy's other books are out of print but may be found in libraries or by searching used book shops. Look especially for *Loaves and Fishes*, her own history of the Catholic Worker movement, *House of Hospitality* and *Therese*, Dorothy's book about St. Therese of Lisieux.

Dorothy Day: Selected Writings, edited and with an introduction by Robert Ellsberg, published by Orbis Books (first published by Alfred A. Knopf as *By Little and By Little*) brings together a great deal of material that would otherwise be hard to find, including a substantial extract from *Therese*, an important work in better understanding Dorothy's approach to prayer and her commitment to "the little way."

Dorothy Day: A Radical Devotion by Robert Coles (Addison-Wesley, 1987) centers on Coles's taped conversations with Dorothy over a period of years. Reading the book is like sipping cup after cup of tea with Dorothy and talking about the most important things in life. If you can find a copy, there is also Coles's *A Spectacle Unto the World* (Viking, 1973); the text is accompanied by Jon Erikson's wonderful photos of Dorothy and the New York Catholic Worker community.

Easy Essays by Peter Maurin, one of the key Catholic Worker books, is back in print thanks to the Franciscan Herald Press. This edition is beautifully illustrated by Ade Bethune.

Voices From the Catholic Worker, compiled and edited by Rosalie Riegle Troester (Temple University Press, 1993) is a massive outpouring of voices that bring both the past and present of the Catholic Worker movement, including controversies still boiling within and between CW communities, vividly to life. A wonderful new addition to the Catholic Worker library.

Fritz Eichenberg: Works of Mercy (Orbis Books, 1993) gathers Fritz's Catholic Worker art as well as texts from Dorothy, Fritz, Robert Ellsberg, and myself. For those who couldn't read *The Catholic Worker*, Fritz's wood engravings said it all.

The other great Catholic Worker artist was Ade Bethune. *Proud Donkey of Schaerbeek* by Judith Stoughton (North Start Press, 1988) tells Ade's life story while also reprinting the artwork so well known to *Catholic Worker* readers.

A Penny a Copy: Readings from The Catholic Worker (Macmillan, 1968), edited by Tom Cornell and myself, provides a sampling of what was published in *The Catholic Worker* in its first thirty-five years. Now out of print, an updated edition is forthcoming from Orbis.

William Miller has written several Catholic Worker books: *A Harsh and Dreadful*

Love (Liverwright, 1973), his history of the Catholic Worker, is my favorite. There is also *Dorothy Day: A Biography* (Harper & Row, 1982), which concentrates on the first half of Dorothy's life, and *All Is Grace: The Spirituality of Dorothy Day* (Doubleday, 1987), which draws on Dorothy's journals.

Catholic Worker Houses: Ordinary Miracles by Sheila Durkin Dierks and Patricia Powers Ladley (Sheed & Ward, 1988) is a portrait in word and picture of seven Catholic Worker communities.

A Revolution of the Heart, edited by Patrick Coy (Temple University Press, 1988; New Society, 1993) is a solid collection of essays on the Catholic Worker movement gathered together by a long-time participant.

Breaking Bread: The Catholic Worker and the Origins of Catholic Radicalism in America (Temple University Press, 1982), by Mel Piehl, is a scholarly work of value for those who want to better understand the role the Catholic Worker played in moving the American Catholic Church from uncritical support of U.S. power to a more significant engagement in peace and justice work.

Peter Maurin: Prophet of the Twentieth Century (Paulist Press, 1981), by Marc Ellis, is both a biography and a work of reflection on the ideas of Peter Maurin, cofounder of the Catholic Worker. The same author has written an account of life with the Catholic Worker community in New York: *A Year at the Catholic Worker* (Paulist Press, 1978).

"Dorothy Day and the Permanent Revolution" (Benet Press) is an attractively illustrated booklet by one of Dorothy's closest friends and collaborators, Eileen Egan, through whom Dorothy came to know Mother Theresa. (Available from Pax Christi USA, 348 E. 10th St., Erie, PA 16503.)

Dorothy Day and the Catholic Worker (State University of New York Press, 1984), by Nancy Roberts, focuses on the history of the newspaper. The author includes in her study material on the FBI investigation of Dorothy and the Catholic Worker movement.

Wings of the Dawn is an autobiography by the court jester of the Catholic Worker, Stanley Vishnewski, who came to visit and never left. (Available from the New York Catholic Worker community; see address below.)

The Dorothy Day Book (Templegate), edited by Margaret Quigley and Michael Garvey, is a collection of some of Dorothy's favorite quotations from other writers plus a few of her own. A small book beautifully illustrated by Ade Bethune linocuts.

Cards and posters of Dorothy Day are available from *U.S. Catholic* and *Salt* magazines (205 W. Monroe, Chicago, IL 60606); Claretian Fathers and Brothers, the magazines' publisher, is working for the canonization of Dorothy Day by the Catholic Church.

Keep in mind that the Catholic Worker movement is at least as vital today as it was when Dorothy Day was alive. A list of Catholic Worker communities — 130 strong at present, including three in Europe — forms an appendix to Rosalie Riegle Troester's *Voices From the Catholic Worker*. A still more up-to-date list can be obtained from the Catholic Worker in New York (Maryhouse, 55 East 3rd. St, New York, NY 10003). While writing, subscribe to *The Catholic Worker*. The price remains 25 cents a year, but it would do you no harm and the Catholic Worker some good if you sent as much as you paid for this book, or even more.

There are in fact many Catholic Worker publications, as each community produces its own. One of the best, *The Catholic Agitator*, comes from the Los Angeles Catholic Worker (632 North Brittania St., Los Angeles, CA 90033).

The Catholic Worker, however, is found neither in books nor newspapers but in houses of hospitality. Go and see for yourself . . .

Index